Intelligent Business

Coursebook

Intermediate
Business English

D1347966

| Tonya Trappe | Graham Tullis |

Pearson Education Limited
Edinburgh Gate
Harlow
Essex CM20 2JE
England
and Associated Companies throughout the world.

www.longman.com

© Pearson Education Limited 2005

First published 2005
Sixth impression 2010
ISBN 978-0-582-84796-5

Set in Economist Roman 10.5 / 12.5

Printed in China
CTPSC/06

Acknowledgements

The authors would like to thank our editors, Ian Wood and Stephen Nicholl, and the following people and organisations for their assistance: Kris Neymarc, Régis Faucon, Julien Griffon, Laurence Baierlein, Gilles Béguin, Henriette Tullis, Sarah Hamberg, Anne Attanasio, Olivier Dexheimer, Jean Pierre Masson, Michel Foucré, Insead Fontainebleau and Harvard Business School. We would also like to thank the students and staff at ESIEA Paris, Pôle universitaire Léonard de Vinci and L'université de Paris XII.

The publishers would like to thank the following people for their help in piloting and developing this course: Irene Barrall, UK; Richard Booker and Karen Ngeow, University of Hong Kong; Louise Bulloch, Intercom Language Services GmbH, Hamburg; Steve Bush, The British Institute Florence; William Cooley, Open Schools of Languages, Madrid; Peter Dunn, Groupe ESC Dijon, Bourgogne; Adolfo Escuder, EU Estudios Empresariales, University of Zaragoza; Wendy Farrar, Università Cattolica del Sacro Cuore, Piacenza; Andrew Hopgood, Linguarama, Hamburg; Ann-Marie Hadzima, Dept of Foreign Languages, National Taiwan University, Taiwan; Samuel C. M. Hsieh, English Department, Chinese Culture University, Taipei; Laura Lewin, ABS International, Buenos Aires; Maite Padrós, Universitat de Barcelona; Louise Pile, UK; Jolanta Korc-Migon, Warsaw; Giuliete Aymard Ramos Siqueira, Sao Paulo; Richmond Stroupe, World Language Center, Soka University, Tokyo; Michael Thompson, Centro Linguistico Università Commerciale L. Bocconi, Milan; Krisztina Tüll, Európai Nyelvek Stúdiója, Budapest.

The publishers are grateful to The Economist for permission to adapt copyright material on pages 9 (©2002), 17 (©2003), 35 (©2003), 43 (©2003), 51 (©2001), 70 (©2003), 87 (©2003), 103 (©2002), 121 (©2003). All articles copyright of The Economist Newspaper Limited. All rights reserved.

We are also grateful to the following for permission to reproduce copyright material:

Gruner & Jahr USA Publishing for extracts from "A Full House" by William Breen first published in Fast Company Magazine, January 2001 and "Failure is Glorious" by Ian Wylie October 2001, both © 2001 Gruner & Jahr USA Publishing, reprinted with permission; and Business Week for extracts by Robert D Hof published in Business Week Magazine December 3rd 2001 and by Pete Engario, Aaron Bernstein and Manjeet Kripalani published in Business Week Magazine February 3rd 2003; Nike for page 25.

Photograph acknowledgements

A1 Pix for pages 20, 80, 94 top right; Ace Stock for pages 71, 74; Apple for pages 27, 127, 131 top right, cover centre; Alamy for pages 43 inset, 55 right, 56, 94 top left, 124; Alessi/Wier Willats Associates for pages 128 bottom, 129 top; Art Directors & TRIP for page 115; Associated Press for page 131 top left; Bellagio for page 75; Britvic Soft Drinks Ltd for page 50 (Pepsi); Camera Press for pages 125, 140 bottom; Corbis for pages 9, 10 top left, 14, 22, 26, 41, 42, 43 right, 46, 47, 51, 85 (Reuters), 86, 97, 101, 103, 128 top middle left, 131 bottom left, cover left and right; Tim Cottingham for page 99; DK Picture Library/Bellagio for pages 76, 77, 82; eBay Inc for page 95 bottom; easyJet Airline Company for page 10 bottom left and bottom right; The Economist for page 43 left; Ecoscene/Barry Hughes for page 144 top left; Empics/Neal Simpson for page 17; Energizer for page 54; Ferretti for page 49; Freeplay/Splash Communications for page 131 top middle and bottom middle; Getty for pages 33 (Illustration Works), 52 (Stone), 94 bottom left (Stone), 123 (Image Bank), 128 top right (Hulton Archive); Image Source for pages 117, 133; Image State for pages 78, 106; J C Mandarin Hotel, Shanghai for page 28; Jaguar Cars for page 50; L'Oreal for pages 50 (Garnier) and 54; OK Magazine for page 92 top; PA Photos for pages 10 top right, 35, 36, 38, 54 (Apple), 67, 69, 72, 87, 90, 102, 104, 108 right, 126, 138 bottom, 144 bottom left, 144 bottom right; Panos Pictures/Fernando Moleres for page 60; Pearson Education for pages 55 left and middle, 94 bottom right and 131 bottom right; Photofusion for page 91; Philips Electronics Ltd for page 31; Picture Desk/Columbia/Kobal Collection for page 30; Powerstock for pages 11, 12; Punchstock/Digital Vision for pages 100, 122, /Image 100 for pages 39, 65, 134, /PhotoDisc for page 34 left; Reporters Archives, Belgium for page 70; Reuters for page 95 top; Rex Features for pages, 15, 25, 45, 62, 66, 88, 92 bottom, 94 middle, 108 left, 118, 129 bottom, 137, 140 top, 144 top right; A. Salah for page 6; Science & Society Picture Library for page 128 top middle right (Science Museum) and top left (National Museum Photography Film & TV); South American Pictures/Tony Morrison for page 48; Sporting Pictures for page 16; Stockbyte for page 34 right; Regis Sultan for page 64; Telegraph.co.uk for page 138 top; Zefa for page 107.

We have been unable to trace the copyright holder of the American Express logo on page 54 and would welcome any information enabling us to do so.

Front cover images supplied by Corbis (left and right) and Apple (centre).

Picture Research by Hilary Luckcock.

Illustration acknowledgements

Kevin Kallagher for 7, 53, 54, 59, 95, 119 and 121; John Stainton for 23 and 111.

Designed by Luke Kelly and Wooden Ark

Contents

Company structure
A matter of choice
The world of lifetime employment in large hierarchical and bureaucratic organisations may be dead, but where is the modern company taking us? A new generation of online companies and networked entrepreneurs is forcing the survivors of the industrial age to merge into giant companies as powerful as nation states. But in an uncertain world only the fittest will survive. **Page 9.**

Fear and management
Terrorising the talent
The football dressing room may be the last refuge of old-style management techniques, but when Britain's most beautiful and skilful footballer was photographed with a wound above his eye inflicted by his manager, the nation asked 'Does fear really motivate?' **Page 17.**

Marketing brands
Seducing the masses
Once a simple guarantee of quality, brands now appeal to emotions and represent aspirations of a better lifestyle. In the new global economy they represent a huge portion of the value of a company, but are increasingly cynical and brand-weary customers seduced by this approach? **Page 51.**

Learning to write well in a foreign language is one of the most difficult challenges facing the language learner. This pocket-sized style guide will help you find the right words, use an appropriate style and write effectively. **See inside the back cover.**

Fair trade

Of celebrities, charity and trade

It is not every day that US finance ministers spend time in African slums discussing development economics with rock stars. Politicians may not always do what voters want but the trip to Uganda by US Treasury Secretary Paul O'Neill shows they certainly listen to public opinion. So if charities want politicians to be nice to Africa, they must persuade voters to demand this. And to attract voters' attention, it helps to have a few celebrities. **Page 103.**

As business English teachers, we know how important it is to learn the key business language necessary to participate in an increasingly international work environment. We also recognise the need to learn about business concepts, developments in business and how business works in different cultures. We are therefore delighted to have written *Intelligent Business* in partnership with The Economist magazine, a unique resource of insights into news and business throughout the world.

Key business concepts

When selecting topics we were very aware of the need to include not only general business areas such as company structures and marketing but also more serious and complex issues such as logistics and finance. We also chose controversial issues such as executive pay and counterfeiting and topics with a wider economic perspective such as lobbies and the developing economies. The result, we feel, is a unique overview of business today that gives students both an opportunity to see key language in context and to expand their business knowledge and horizons.

Language development

The exercises developed around the central theme of each unit give ample opportunities to review and practice important grammar and vocabulary in both spoken and written contexts. Furthermore, the career skills syllabus develops the key communicative language and strategies necessary to succeed in today's work environment. All of these are then put to use in the end of unit problem-solving task.

The *Intelligent Business* intermediate Coursebook is accompanied by a separate Workbook that provides comprehensive self-study language practice along with a complete Cambridge BEC Vantage practice exam. There is also the *Intelligent Business* intermediate Skills Book: a task-driven intensive course that practises key language from the *Intelligent Business* syllabus through authentic business tasks. All of these components are covered by a single Teacher's Book.

Both the Coursebook and the Skills Book can be supplemented with the *Intelligent Business* intermediate video: a drama illustrating the key language and business skills common to both Coursebook and Skills Book. In addition, there is the www.intelligent-business.org website which contains further information on the course, downloadable resources, teacher support and premium content from the www.economist.com website.

Our intention when writing *Intelligent Business* was to make a truly contemporary world of business accessible to learners of business English – whatever their level of world and business knowledge. We hope you will find that it does so. If it is both enjoyable and beneficial to users we will have completed our task.

We wish you every success in your future English-speaking working lives!

Tonya Trappe
Graham Tullis

Survival of the fittest

Keynotes

There are many different types of companies. Most large corporations are public limited or **joint-stock** companies, which means that **shareholders** who wish to invest in the company can buy and sell parts of the company on the stock exchange. Many are **multinationals** with **subsidiaries** and **assets** in various different countries and they generally engage in **mergers** with other companies and **acquisitions** in order to expand. However, the large corporation is increasingly under threat from the growing number of **dotcoms** set up by **entrepreneurs**.

Types of company

1 Which of the following types of companies would you prefer to work for? What are the advantages and disadvantages of working for each one?

- a large multinational corporation
- a small or medium-sized family business
- a trendy new high-tech corporation

2 Read the list of developments that threaten the survival of the traditional company. What are the positive or negative impacts on companies of each one?

- developments in technology
- growth in the power of consumer groups
- expansion of e-business
- increase in shareholder power
- financial scandals
- transfer of money and jobs to cheaper countries
- weakening trade unions

Job losses to India

STOLEN JOBS?

Stock market crashes

The end of the tycoon?

Parmalat, accounting scandal

Company structure

Reading **1** Read the text on the opposite page and say why the author thinks 'choice' will play a major role in determining the structure of tomorrow's companies.

2 Read the text again and answer the following questions.

1 What were the characteristics of US corporations in the past?
2 What changes have occurred to those corporations?
3 What is meant by 'shifting from high-volume to high-value'?
4 What different types of future companies does the author mention?
5 Why does he believe there is not one definite type of future company?
6 What does he believe to be the key to survival for companies in future?

Speaking Would you prefer to be a freelance worker or employed with a fixed salary? What are the advantages and disadvantages of each situation?

Glossary

durable long-lasting

decade 10 years

tangible assets buildings, machinery, etc.

BrE vs AmE English

-ise / -ize

standardise (BrE)

standardize (AmE)

Company Structure

A matter of choice

That reliable workhorse of capitalism – the joint-stock company looks surprisingly durable. But pressure on it is increasing.

In 1967, John Kenneth Galbraith's *The New Industrial State* argued that the USA was run by a handful of big companies who planned the economy in the name of stability.

These were hierarchical and bureaucratic organizations making long runs of standardised products. They introduced "new and improved" varieties with predictable regularity; they provided their workers with lifetime employment and they enjoyed fairly good industrial relations with the giant trade unions.

That world is now dead. The US's giant corporations have either disappeared or been transformed by global competition. Most have shifted their production systems from high-volume to high-value, from standardised to customised. And they have flattened their management hierarchies. Few people these days expect to spend their lives moving up the ladder of a single organization. Dramatic changes are taking place. But where exactly are they taking us? Where is the modern company heading?

There are three standard answers to this question. The first is that a handful of giant companies are engaged in a "silent takeover" of the world. The past couple of decades have seen a record number of mergers. The survivors, it is maintained, are far more powerful than nation states.

The second school of thought argues almost the opposite: it says that big companies are a thing of the past. For a glimpse of the future, look at the Monorail Corporation, which sells computers. Monorail owns no factories, warehouses or any other tangible assets. It operates from a single floor that it leases in an office building in Atlanta. Freelance workers are designing the computers while demand is still low.

The third school of thought says that companies are being replaced by "networks". Groups of entrepreneurs form such a network to market an idea. They then sell it to the highest bidder and move on to produce another idea and to create another firm, with the money being supplied all the time by venture capitalists.

Another way to look at the future of the company is to focus on the environment that will determine it. That environment is dominated by one thing: choice. Technology and globalisation open up ever more opportunities for individuals and firms to collect information and conduct economic activity outside traditional structures. While the age of mass production lowered the costs of products at the expense of limiting choices, modern "flexible" production systems both lower costs and increase choice. Consumers have more choice over where they spend their money. Producers have more choice over which suppliers to use. Shareholders have more choice over where to put their money. With all that choice around, future companies will have to be very flexible in order to quickly adapt to the changing environments if they are to survive ■

1 **Find the words in the text to describe people who:**

1 work independently or on short-term contracts
2 are willing to take risks
3 are willing to invest in new and/or risky business projects
4 express a wish to buy something
5 make goods
6 own part of a company

2 **Match the words with the definitions.**

1 bureaucracy   a goods of the same quality and design
2 flattened hierarchy   b inflexible system of administration
3 standardised products   c rent a building on a temporary basis
4 lifetime employment   d more middle than senior managers
5 merger   e buildings and machinery a company owns
6 customised   f permanent jobs
7 tangible assets   g made for a particular user
8 lease   h when two companies become one

3 **Which of the following types of company do the words from exercises 1 and 2 refer to?**

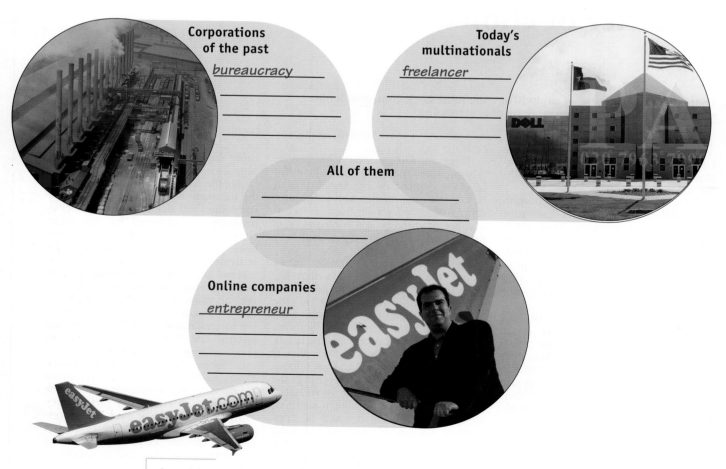

Corporations of the past

bureaucracy
_____
_____
_____

Today's multinationals

freelancer
_____
_____
_____

All of them

_____
_____
_____

Online companies

entrepreneur
_____
_____
_____

Can you think of examples of these company types?

Present simple and continuous

1 Complete the rules below with *simple* or *continuous*.

The present _____ describes
a facts that will not change
b regular events and processes
c a scheduled event

The present _____ describes
d things happening now
e temporary situations
f future arrangements

Note: The continuous is usually not used with the following:

– ownership (*have*, *want*, *need*, etc.)
– sense (*look*, *sound*, *feel*, etc.)
– emotion / opinion (*like*, *love*, *hate*, *think*, *believe*, etc.)
– routines (*usually*, *always*, *sometimes*, etc.)

For more information see page 157.

2 Match the following examples with the rules a–f.

1 The first answer isn't a very positive one.   *simple (a)*
2 Dramatic changes are taking place in company structure.
3 They then sell it to the highest bidder and move on to a new idea.
4 Business doesn't start on the stock exchange until tomorrow at 9 am.
5 Freelance workers are designing the computers while demand is low.
6 Is he meeting the shareholders on Monday?

Practice   **Complete the text below with the appropriate form of the present simple or continuous.**

Will the corporation survive?

Since the corporation was invented it has been widely accepted that bringing activities together into one large company (^{1}lower) _lowers_ 'transactional' and communication costs, and that suppliers and manufacturers (^{2}have) _____ market power due to their knowledge of markets. However, nowadays the internet (^{3}eliminate) _____ the physical costs of communication. As a result it (^{4}become) _____ more profitable to outsource many activities. Power (^{5}shift) _____ to the customer who could be either another business or the end-user.

All this raises two burning questions. Firstly, (^{6}it / mean) _____ that the supplier will no longer be the seller but become the buyer for the customer? Secondly, (^{7}diversification / change) _____ the structure of companies? The answer to both questions at the moment, is *yes* for many business sectors. Some of the US's largest pharmaceutical companies (^{8}not / manufacture) _____ drugs themselves anymore. During this transition period, they (^{9}wholesale) _____ every other kind of pharmacy product as well. At the annual conference for managers in the pharmaceutical sector, which (^{10}take place) _____ next month, the main topic will surely be what to outsource to smaller companies next.

Speaking   **Work in pairs. Find out about a typical day at work/the weekend for your partner and what he/she has planned for next week.**

Companies and careers

1 Study the two very different company structures below. Which type of company, mentioned in the text on page 9, does each of these structures represent?

Transatlantica, Inc.

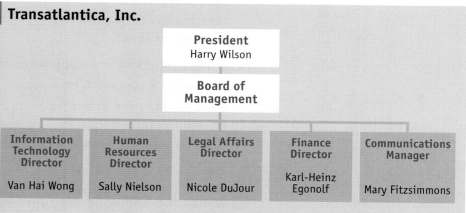

| President
Harry Wilson |
| Board of
Management |

Information Technology Director	Human Resources Director	Legal Affairs Director	Finance Director	Communications Manager
Van Hai Wong	Sally Nielson	Nicole DuJour	Karl-Heinz Egonolf	Mary Fitzsimmons

Spearhead Electronics Ltd.

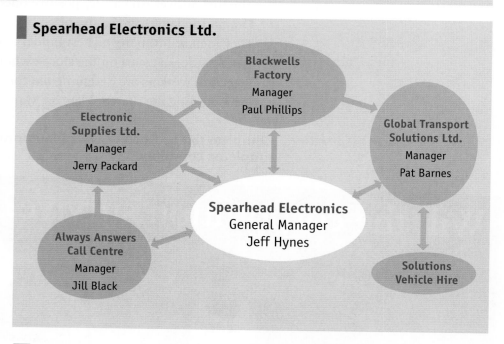

Blackwells Factory — Manager Paul Phillips

Electronic Supplies Ltd. — Manager Jerry Packard

Global Transport Solutions Ltd. — Manager Pat Barnes

Spearhead Electronics General Manager Jeff Hynes

Always Answers Call Centre — Manager Jill Black

Solutions Vehicle Hire

2 Look at the structures again and answer the questions.

At Transatlantica, Inc., which division or department deals with

1 computer programming and software?
2 trade unions?
3 new accounting principles?
4 patents for new products?

At Spearhead Electronics Ltd.,

5 which company provides parts to another?
6 what is the name of the company in the logistics sector?
7 which companies are in the services sector?
8 who is in charge of the manufacturing company?
9 which company is a subsidiary?

Talking about your job

When meeting people for the first time in both professional and social situations it is common to exchange information about your job. The following phrases are useful for describing what you do.

My job entails/involves ...   *I'm in charge of ...*

I'm responsible for ...   *I report to ...*

I work for/under ...   *I manage ...*

Listen to several people from the companies on the opposite page talking about their jobs and complete the following table. Which of the above phrases do you hear?

	name	duties	no. of workers	phrases used
1	Jeff Hynes	liaising /dealing with other companies	5 project managers	my job involves ...
2				
3				
4				
5				

Look at the job profile below. Write similar profiles for the people in the listening activity above.

Name: Van Hai Wong

Present position: Director of Information technology at Transatlantica, Inc.

Present responsibilities: In charge of a team of 25 people, who purchase and maintain all company IT hardware and services.

Using the profiles, take it in turns to role-play introducing yourself and talking about your job.

Hierarchy

Some cultures prefer steep hierarchies with many levels of management, clear roles and very powerful senior managers. Others prefer flat hierarchies with more equality and flexibility. What is common in your country? Which would you prefer to work in? Why?

Dilemma & Decision

Dilemma: The virtue of necessity

Brief

A serious safety problem is threatening the future of Transal, a pipeline company. Hundreds of yearly accidents have led to high absenteeism, causing lost time, low morale, unsatisfactory efficiency levels, falling profits and a falling share price. Press articles about the company's lack of concern for its employees are having a very negative effect on customers, shareholders and staff. If the company is to survive it must develop a 'safety conscious culture'. The question is: how?

Task 1

Look at the three options open to Transal and discuss the potential benefits and disadvantages of each one.

1   **The International School of Industrial Engineering**

    Send all technical staff members on an intensive 'safety awareness' course run by a high-profile school of engineering. The course is very expensive but has an excellent reputation. This will be emphasised at a press conference organised to announce the new company plans. On their return, the managers will train their teams. The forecast is to have improved safety conditions by this time next year.

2   **Stanford, Traynor & Weldon Associates.**

    Bring outside consultants into every subsidiary to organise training schemes for all employees over a period of six months. This would be more expensive but would give low-level workers an opportunity to speak to experts and to point out problems. The results should be almost immediate and the experts would be on hand to talk to the press.

3   **Safety Charity Challenge**

    Offer to give a sum of money to a community charity of the workers' choice every time they eliminate a safety hazard. An untested idea suggested by the communications department. If successful, it could lead to a lot of positive publicity and be very cost-effective. However, it relies on the employees' willingness to take part in such a scheme. There is no knowing how long it might take to improve conditions.

Task 2

Choose the best option and present your arguments to the class.

Write it up

Write a brief email to the Transal board recommending the best option and giving reasons for your decision. (See Style guide, p18.)

Decision:

Turn to page 141 and see what happened when a famous British company was faced with the same dilemma.

Unit 2
Leadership

www.longman-elt.com   www.economist.com

Terrorising the talent

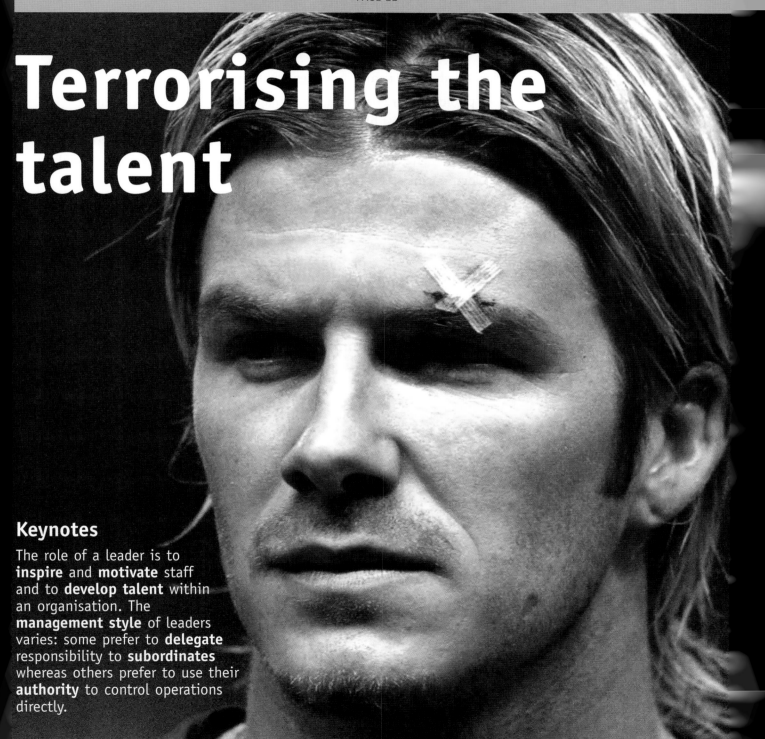

Keynotes

The role of a leader is to **inspire** and **motivate** staff and to **develop talent** within an organisation. The **management style** of leaders varies: some prefer to **delegate** responsibility to **subordinates** whereas others prefer to use their **authority** to control operations directly.

Management styles

Opinions differ about what is the best way to manage and motivate employees. Which of the following statements do you agree with? Discuss your views with a partner.

a   Employees cannot be trusted and must therefore be closely supervised.

b   Staff should be allowed to organise their own work.

c   The best motivation is money and recognition for meeting targets.

Fear and management

1 **Read the text about leadership on the opposite page. What motivation techniques are mentioned?**

2 **Read the text again. Are these statements true or false?**

1   A photographer witnessed the manager kicking David Beckham.

2   The manager lost his temper because the team lost the match.

3   Management tactics are easier to identify in business than in sport.

4   Patterson encouraged his employees to make themselves indispensable.

5   When business is good, fear is used less as a management tactic.

6   Fear may help some people to reach their targets.

7   Both company employees and artists share the same fear of failure.

3 **What fears make people work hard? Can fear motivate people as successfully as rewarding them?**

Synonyms

1 **Match the words from the text with similar meanings.**

1	inspire	a	technique
2	fire	b	terror
3	fear	c	motivate
4	defeat	d	employee
5	upset	e	sack
6	subordinate	f	failure
7	tactic	g	hurt

Management

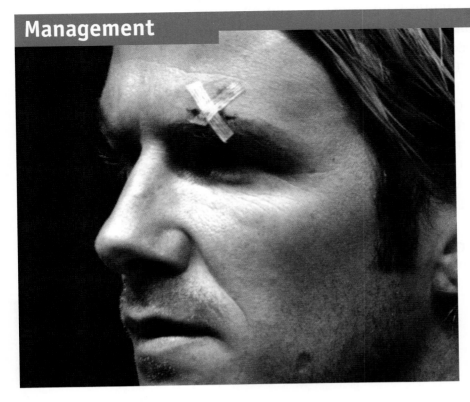

Glossary

indispensable can't do without it

emotional kick feeling of excitement

neurotic in a state of anxiety

fragile egos very sensitive people

Fear and management

When to terrorise talent

The football dressing room remains the last refuge of old-style management techniques.

The nation was in shock. David Beckham, Britain's most beautiful (and skilful) footballer emerged from his house on Monday morning to allow the world to photograph a wound above his left eye. Sir Alex Ferguson, manager of his then team Manchester United, had lost his temper after a defeat and kicked a football boot, which hit the Beckham eyebrow.

In sports, more than in most businesses, the management tactics are out in the open for all to see. Not many managers try to strangle their subordinates – as Bobby Knight, a former basketball coach at Indiana University, once did. But the ability to inspire fear has always been an essential tool of management.

Lots of successful chief executives rule by terror. None, it must be said, reaches the standard set by John Patterson, who built NCR early in the 20th century. "When a man gets indispensable, let's fire him," he would apparently say. One NCR executive discovered he had been fired when he found his desk and chair in flames on the company lawn. Modern laws on constructive dismissal and employee harassment have put an end to such fun.

However, terror in the workplace is making a comeback these days. In an economic upswing, fear goes underground. Workers are scarce, and therefore powerful; bosses must handle the talent with care. When times turn tough, the balance of power swings. As Hank Paulson, chairman of Goldman Sachs, put it, in a speech that upset his staff, "in almost every one of our businesses, there are 15–20% of the people that really add 80% of the value." In other words, 80–85% are largely redundant – and had better shape up fast.

Motivating talent

Does fear really motivate? In sport says Scott Snook, who teaches organizational behaviour at Harvard Business School, "fear can become a barrier to taking risks, yet can provide the essential emotional kick needed to meet a challenge." Coaches need to strike the right balance (and the right player?) in order to develop talent.

Yet used in the boardroom, fear can be disastrous. Tony Couchman, a headhunter at Egon Zehnder in London, recalls the board of a large firm with a chief executive who so dominated his directors that they rarely questioned or challenged him. "Success in such a company depends on having a great leader and a steady market," he argues.

Jim Collins, author of a book that explains why some firms succeed in making the jump "from good to great" and others fail, found that the approach to fear was a key distinction among firms that he surveyed. He found that in the truly successful firms people were "productively neurotic". At Microsoft, for example, employees worry all year at the prospect of their annual meetings with Bill Gates, where even being shouted at would not hurt as much as seeming to be an idiot.

The driving fear of failure, points out Mr Collins, is not unique to corporate life. "I'm self-employed, and I live with constant fear," he says. "But I'm self-afraid." That kind of fear is common among creative artists and also in professional services where the person is the product and lots of fragile egos have to be managed ■

2 Complete the sentences with the words below.

manager   subordinates   coach   chief executive (CEO)
workers   staff   directors   employee

1   The new _manager_ improved morale in the department.
2   The _____ praised his team upon reaching the Cup Final.
3   Our board of _____ meets every three months to discuss strategy.
4   The factory _____ went on strike because of low pay.
5   The share price went up when the new _____ was appointed.
6   I have to do the appraisals for the six _____ who report to me.
7   An aggressive management style led to an increase in _____ turnover.
8   Every _____ in the company gets health and safety training.

3 Complete the article with words from exercises 1 and 2. Sometimes more than one answer is possible.

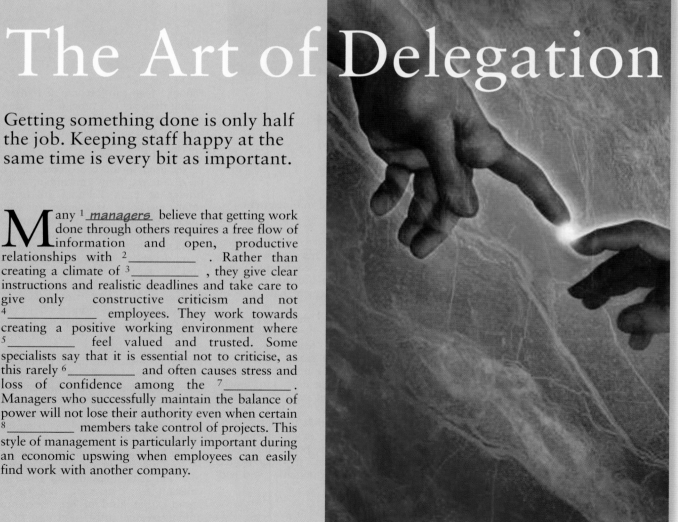

The Art of Delegation

Getting something done is only half the job. Keeping staff happy at the same time is every bit as important.

Many [1] _managers_ believe that getting work done through others requires a free flow of information and open, productive relationships with [2]_____ . Rather than creating a climate of [3]_____ , they give clear instructions and realistic deadlines and take care to give only constructive criticism and not [4]_____ employees. They work towards creating a positive working environment where [5]_____ feel valued and trusted. Some specialists say that it is essential not to criticise, as this rarely [6]_____ and often causes stress and loss of confidence among the [7]_____ . Managers who successfully maintain the balance of power will not lose their authority even when certain [8]_____ members take control of projects. This style of management is particularly important during an economic upswing when employees can easily find work with another company.

Speaking   **In what ways can successful leaders win the respect of subordinates and exercise authority over them?**

Collocations

1 Match each of the following verbs with one set of nouns.

set	meet	make	take

1 _____ a chance
an opportunity
a position
a point

2 _____ a deadline
a need
the cost
expectations

3 _____ a mistake
a judgement
a profit/loss
a call

4 _____ a precedent
an example
an objective
a limit

2 Use some of the collocations to complete the dialogues below.

1 a Are you sure these figures are correct? They look a little high to me.
b You're right. I think I _____ a _____ in the calculations.

2 a What do you think of their proposal?
b Too risky. We can't _____ a _____ on an unknown supplier.

3 a They say they absolutely must have the final version by Friday.
b We'll never be able to _____ a _____ like that!

4 a It's the first time we've agreed to pay expenses on a project like this.
b Yes, I know. I hope this won't _____ a _____ that we'll regret later.

5 a I'm not sure if we should sell now or wait until the market improves.
b Yeah. It's difficult to know which would be the best _____ to _____ .

6 a It looks like we've used almost all of the budget.
b Right. We're going to have to _____ a tight _____ on spending from now on.

1 David Hargreaves is the HR manager at Radius Group. You will hear him talk about managing people. Before you listen, answer these questions.

1 Do you think there is a secret to successful leadership?

2 Do you think that life inside an organisation is in any way similar to life inside a family? If so, in what way?

Now listen and answer the questions.

1 How does David motivate his staff?

2 How does he monitor progress?

3 Why does he arrive early at work?

4 How does his team make decisions?

5 What does David think the secret of leadership is?

Work in pairs. Tell your partner about a very good manager or teacher you have known. What made him/her special?

Articles

Read the extract below and underline all the nouns. Which nouns are preceded by indefinite articles *a/an*, the definite article *the* or no article at all?

Does <u>fear</u> really motivate? In sport, says Scott Snook, a teacher in organisational behaviour at Harvard Business School, (one of the most famous business schools in the world) 'fear can become a barrier to taking risks, yet can provide the essential emotional kick needed to meet a challenge. Coaches need to strike the right balance in order to develop talent.'

The indefinite article *a/an* refers to

- non-specific singular countable nouns (*He's **a** good **manager**.*)
- jobs and nouns of nationality (*I'm **a sales executive**.*)

The definite article *the* refers to

- nouns already mentioned or specified (*I gave **the report** to her.*)
- nouns that are one of a kind (*You can read about it on **the internet**.*)
- the superlative form of adjectives (*It's **the best** job I've had.*)

There is usually no article with

- general plural and uncountable nouns (***Criticism** doesn't help.*)
- abstract nouns such as *talent, success* (*We should develop our **talent**.*)

For more information, see page 157.

Practice **Complete the following article with either a definite or indefinite article or no article at all (Ø).**

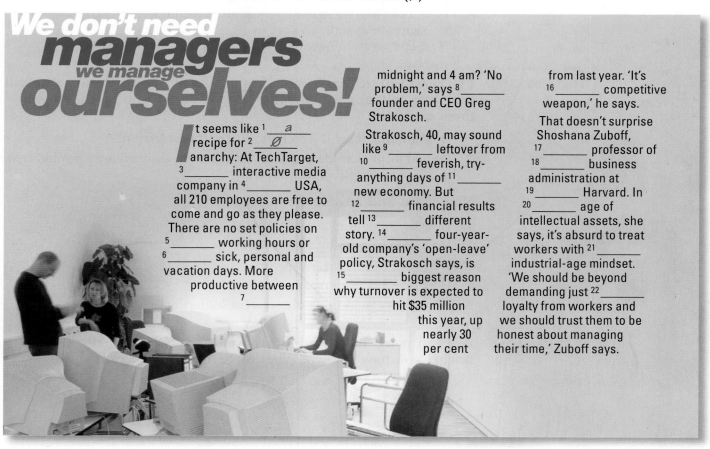

We don't need managers we manage ourselves!

It seems like ¹ __a__ recipe for ² __Ø__ anarchy: At TechTarget, ³ _____ interactive media company in ⁴ _____ USA, all 210 employees are free to come and go as they please. There are no set policies on ⁵ _____ working hours or ⁶ _____ sick, personal and vacation days. More productive between ⁷ _____ midnight and 4 am? 'No problem,' says ⁸ _____ founder and CEO Greg Strakosch.

Strakosch, 40, may sound like ⁹ _____ leftover from ¹⁰ _____ feverish, try-anything days of ¹¹ _____ new economy. But ¹² _____ financial results tell ¹³ _____ different story. ¹⁴ _____ four-year-old company's 'open-leave' policy, Strakosch says, is ¹⁵ _____ biggest reason why turnover is expected to hit $35 million this year, up nearly 30 per cent from last year. 'It's ¹⁶ _____ competitive weapon,' he says.

That doesn't surprise Shoshana Zuboff, ¹⁷ _____ professor of ¹⁸ _____ business administration at ¹⁹ _____ Harvard. In ²⁰ _____ age of intellectual assets, she says, it's absurd to treat workers with ²¹ _____ industrial-age mindset. 'We should be beyond demanding just ²² _____ loyalty from workers and we should trust them to be honest about managing their time,' Zuboff says.

Getting things done

Management is often about getting people to do things effectively and on time. Direct orders can demotivate subordinates as they give them no choice but to do as they are told. A softer approach is to focus on the positive outcome of an employee completing a task:

It would be a great help if you could get the report done by Friday.

By phrasing instructions as questions, an employee feels respected and involved in the decision-making process.

Would you mind working late next week?

1 Listen to the three short dialogues. Which of the following phrases do the speakers use?

Is there any way you can ... ?

I don't suppose you could ... ?

Do you mind ...?

Would you do me a favour and ... ?

I was wondering whether you could ... ?

Would you mind ... -ing?

I'd really appreciate it if you ...

It'd be a great help if you could ...

2 Read the instructions below. How would you rephrase them to make them softer? Practise with a partner.

1 Get it done by Friday.
2 Tell her to come and see me.
3 Mail it to my home address.
4 Don't waste your time on that.
5 Enter all that on the data base.

Look at the following situations. Imagine that you are the person's manager. How would you approach these situations? What would you actually say to the person in each case?

1 Bill Jarvis is a young engineer who has only been with your organisation for four months. He has an independent approach to doing his work. You asked him to hand in a report three days ago. He has not responded to the several emails you sent him to remind him.

2 Janet Feynman is a young junior manager in your department. She gets on with most people in the office. However, she has recently had some conflict with Katia, one of her colleagues. A new project has come up and you need Janet to work on it with Katia.

Being direct

In direct cultures instructions are very short. This can be seen as impolite and aggressive by people from indirect cultures, where instructions are usually polite requests. Can you think of examples of each culture? How might this difference cause misunderstanding in multicultural teams?

Dilemma & Decision

Dilemma: Mission: Impossible?

Brief

Louis Schweitzer, the 59-year-old CEO of the Renault group, has just received the latest results for Nissan, the Japanese car manufacturer in which Renault has a 37 per cent stake. The situation looks bad. Nissan has lost money for the sixth consecutive year, the company's debts have now soared to a record $19 billion and they are now losing $1,000 dollars on every new car they produce. Clearly something needs to be done to return Nissan to profit and quickly. The time has come to appoint a new CEO. There is only one name that comes to Schweitzer's mind: Carlos Ghosn, the tough results-oriented director of Renault's engineering division. He would be just the person for the job. But how to convince him to accept what looks like an impossible mission?

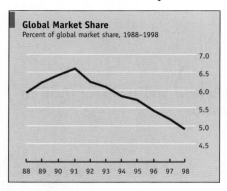

Global Market Share
Percent of global market share, 1988–1998

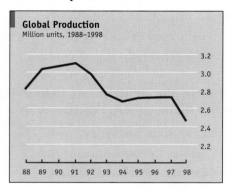

Global Production
Million units, 1988–1998

Task 1

Work in groups. Group A you are Louis Schweitzer (turn to page 143). Group B you are Carlos Ghosn (turn to page 145). Look at the notes on Japanese business culture on page 139. What other cultural factors might affect the success of appointing a foreign CEO at Nissan?

Task 2

Prepare to discuss the assignment to head Nissan. Decide what outcome you want from the discussion and make notes to support your case.

Task 3

Meet the other group and discuss the issues involved in the assignment. Try to reach a satisfactory solution. Make notes on what you discuss.

Write it up

Write an email to the other group with minutes of your discussion. (See Style guide, page 18.)

Decision:

⊙ Listen to Rachel Ellison, a specialist in cross-cultural leadership, commenting on this case.

Useful phrases

It'd be a great help if ...
I'd really appreciate it if ...
Is there any way you can ... ?
Would you mind ... -ing?
I don't suppose you could ... ?

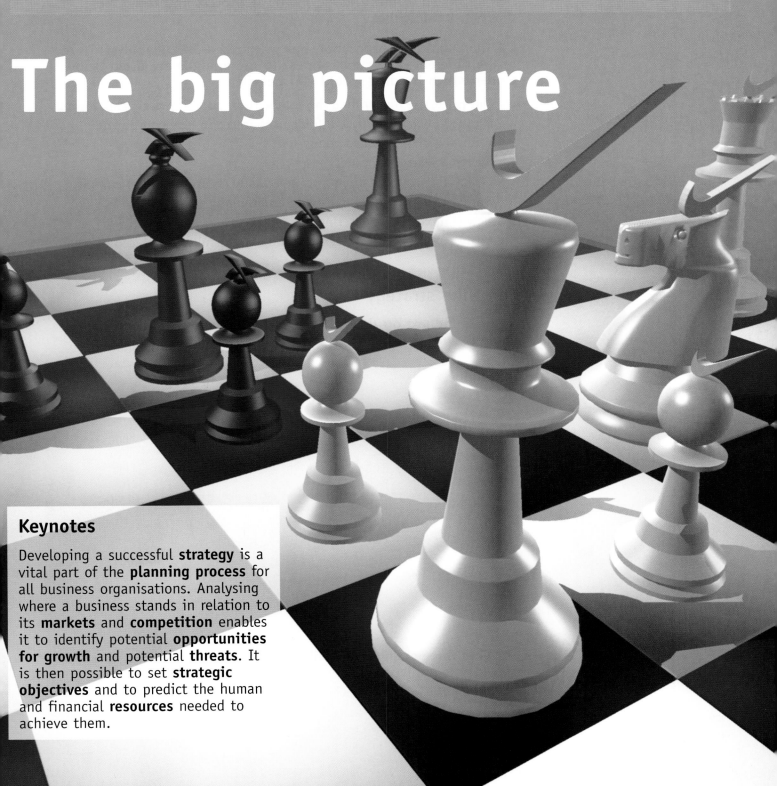

Unit 3
Strategy

www.longman-elt.com   www.economist.com

The big picture

Keynotes

Developing a successful **strategy** is a vital part of the **planning process** for all business organisations. Analysing where a business stands in relation to its **markets** and **competition** enables it to identify potential **opportunities for growth** and potential **threats**. It is then possible to set **strategic objectives** and to predict the human and financial **resources** needed to achieve them.

Choosing a strategy

Which of the following factors do you think a company considers when it undergoes the strategic planning process? Put them in order of importance.

product development   economic forecasts   competitors   technology
human and financial resources   fashions and trends   current sales

1 David Drexler is a professor of economics. Listen to him explain one approach to the strategic planning process and draw the diagram he describes.

2 The Quadrant corporation has prepared a SWOT analysis. Some of the different points that appear in the analysis are listed below. Under which heading would you put them?

1   Our prices are higher than the competition but our margins are lower.
2   Planned EU legislation will force us to invest in new equipment.
3   We have a highly-skilled young staff.
4   We have a strong internet presence.
5   We have discovered a new and potentially cheaper source of supply.
6   Our brands are not recognised internationally.
7   New companies are entering our industry.
8   Analysis shows our products could be successfully introduced in Asia.

The Nike strategy

1 Read the text on the opposite page and complete the SWOT analysis with the different elements of Nike's strategic position.

Strengths	Weaknesses
leader in sports marketing	

Opportunities	Threats

2 What three changes has Nike had to make in its effort to appeal to a female audience?

Nike's Goddess

Could a famously masculine company finally click with female customers? That was the challenge behind Nike Goddess, whose goal was to change how the company designed for, sold to and communicated with women.

In its 30-year history, Nike had become the undisputed leader in sports marketing. But beneath the success was an Achilles' heel. Nike is named after a woman — the Greek goddess of victory — but for most of its history, the company had been perceived as being mostly about men.

Could Nike do more to realise the full potential of female customers? And how could it afford not to, given the threats to its future with Air Jordan running out of air and brands like Skechers digging into the teen market with shoes inspired by skateboarding, not basketball. That was the huge question at Nike HQ. The launch of Nike Goddess was the makings of an answer.

Just Doing It Differently

For much of its history, Nike's destiny was controlled by its founders, Phil Knight and his running buddies, who signed up athletes in locker rooms and made the executive decisions. But by throwing together a diverse team of people with different backgrounds and different levels of seniority, Nike has found that it can keep many of its core attributes while adding new sources of inspiration.

Take the combination of star designer John Hoke and newcomer Mindy Grossman, vice president of global apparel. Hoke designed the look and feel of the first Nike Goddess store. Then Grossman, whose career has included helping make Ralph Lauren into a retail icon, pitched the design ideas to Nike's top retailers as stores within stores. Now it looks like Nike has a chance to reach a crucial objective: double its sales to women by the end of the decade.

How to Sell to Women

Nike Goddess began as a concept for a women-only store, and there's a reason why. Many of the retail settings in which the company's products were found were a turnoff to female customers: dark, loud, and harsh – in a word, male. In sharp contrast, the Nike Goddess stores have the comforting feel of a woman's own home.

How to Design for Women

Designing a new approach to retail was only one element in Nike's campaign. Another was redesigning the shoes and clothes themselves. Nike's footwear designers worked on 18-month production cycles – which made it hard to stay in step with the new styles and colours for women. The apparel group, which worked around 12-month cycles, was better at keeping up with fashion trends. But that meant that the clothes weren't co-ordinated with the shoes – a big turnoff for women.

How to Talk to Women

When Jackie Thomas, Nike's US brand marketing director for women, first heard the phrase 'Nike goddess,' she wasn't impressed. 'I don't like talking to women through gender,' she says. Nike Goddess had to mean something to women and it was her job to make that happen. 'Women don't need anybody's permission. We are at our best when we are showing women a place where they didn't think they could be.' For John Hoke, the real power of Nike Goddess is not about traffic at stores. It's about changing minds inside the company. 'I knew that Goddess could galvanise us,' he says, 'It was an opportunity to redefine and re-energise our entire brand around a market that was taking off.'

Glossary

pitch sales argument

turnoff demotivating factor

galvanise shock into finding a solution

3 Read the text again. Who was responsible for the following?

1 Nike being seen as a male brand
2 taking market share away from Nike
3 creating a new style of Nike retail outlet
4 persuading Nike retailers to accept the Nike Goddess concept
5 putting sports celebrities under contract
6 communicating more effectively with women

Vocabulary 1

1 Replace the *italicised* words with one that has a similar meaning.

1 Nike's destiny was controlled by its *founders* ...
  a designers   b sponsors   c creators

2 The company had an *Achilles' heel.*
  a strongpoint   b secret weapon   c hidden weakness

3 ... a collection of people with different levels of *seniority.*
  a knowledge   b rank   c performance

4 Nike has found that it can keep many of its core *attributes* ...
  a origins   b qualities   c aspects

5 ... vice president of global *apparel* ...
  a clothing   b equipment   c designs

6 Footwear designers worked on 18-month production *cycles.*
  a shifts   b delays   c periods

7 'I knew that Goddess could *galvanise* us.'
  a motivate   b surprise   c renew

Breaking into a new market

Mario Moretti Polegato is the [1] ___founder___ of Geox footwear. In the early 1990s he created a new footwear [2] _____ : a special membrane that could be used in shoes to prevent perspiration. He approached Nike, Adidas, Timberland, the [3] _____ of the footwear market.

But nobody was interested. So he decided to go it alone and set up his company with five employees. Today the company has 2,800 employees and sales of $350m. Mario thinks the company's next [4] _____ will come from the clothing market and he plans to produce a range of clothes incorporating the same patented material. The only [5] _____ that Geox faces is the same for all fashion businesses: a sudden shift in consumer [6] _____ .

2 Complete the text with the following words.

leaders   trends   threat   founder   opportunity   concept

Suffixes

Look at the words from the text on page 25 and how they are formed. How do the suffixes change the form of the word?

1 active [adj] – activ**ist** *noun / person*
2 misery [n] – miser**able**
3 senior [adj] – senior**ity**
4 custom [n] – custom**er**
5 resident [n] – residenti**al**
6 energy [n] – energ**ise**

What affixes can you attach to the following words? How do they change the form of the words? Use a dictionary to help you.

diverse inspire opportune design public
commerce revolution repute comfort retail

1 Look at the MP3 player that has been specifically designed to appeal to women. What features make it appeal to women?

2 Choose one of the following. How do you think they could be made more appealing to women?

computers video games MP3 players football

Future forms

We use different verb forms to talk about the future:

a *The marketing department **is launching** the new campaign this spring.*
b *We **start** the visit with a tour of the Indonesian factory.*
c *I'll **forward** the report to you by email.*
d *There is no doubt in my mind. We **will succeed**.*
e *We're **going to target** a new customer profile.*

Which future forms are used to:

1 make a prediction
2 describe a timetabled event
3 talk about a personal intention
4 talk about an event arranged for a certain time
5 make a spontaneous decision or offer

 For more information, see page 158.

1 Bruce Hector is organising an 'Asian Strategy and Leadership' conference in Shanghai. Listen to his conversation with Naomi Wang, the regional conference manager for Asia and make any necessary changes to the programme details below.

'Taming the tiger – Strategy and Risk in the Asian market'

Yangtze Garden Conference Center, Shanghai.
20 August. Registration fee: $ 1,650

Time	Speaker	Title
09:00	**Dr Alasdair Summerville** President, Orient Automation Systems	**Downturn to Danger?** Market volatility and growth – an assessment
10:00	Coffee break	
10:30	**Alasdair Ross** Riskwire – Economist Intelligence unit	**Risk Radar** Mapping and measuring risk in Asia
12:00	Lunch	
13:30	**Professor Giulietta Bertoni** Milan University	**No Brand's Land** Building brand identity in the Chinese market
15:00	**Jimmy Tan** President, Pacific Assets	**Eastern Promise?** Liberalisation and the single Asian currency bloc
16:00	Coffee break	
16:30	**Dr Summerville, Alasdair Ross,** Professor Bertoni, Jimmy Tan	**Panel discussion and review**

2 Complete Bruce and Naomi's conversation with the appropriate future forms. Then listen again and check your answers.

Naomi Hi, Bruce. It's Naomi here. I'm calling about the conference in Shanghai. We (^{1} have to) _____ make some changes.

Bruce Hi, Naomi. OK, hang on, let me get a pen. Right, fire away.

Naomi I don't think the Yangtze Garden (^{2} be) _____ big enough. We (^{3} need) _____ a centre that can seat at least 600.

Bruce That many? Any suggestions?

Naomi The Mandarin Palace Center (^{4} be) _____ free that day. I've already spoken to them and I (^{5} meet) _____ the conference manager tomorrow. It (^{6} mean) _____ increasing the registration fee by $50 though.

Bruce That (^{7} not / be) _____ a problem. Anything else?

Naomi Alasdair Ross can't do the morning session as his plane (^{8} not / land) _____ until 9:30, so I've arranged things with Jimmy Tan and they (^{9} switch) _____ slots. Also, Milan University say they (^{10} send) _____ Carla Marisco because Professor Bertoni can't make it. But the talk (^{11} be) _____ the same.

Bruce Fine. Make those changes and I (^{12} inform) _____ everyone at my end.

Speaking Work as a class. Prepare a diary for the weekend and write in any arrangements you have. Then try to make more arrangements with as many other people in the class as possible.

Short presentations

The ability to make a short presentation of your ideas is a key business skill that enables you to communicate statistical information, present ideas and persuade people of the strengths of your argument. To do this effectively you need to prepare.

1 Make a plan of your talk. This should include at least three sections:
 - introduction
 - development
 - conclusion

2 Write detailed notes of what you will say, showing
 - key points and keywords
 - transitions between the different sections
 - visual aids you will refer to
 - the action points you will stress

3 Practise your presentation to make sure that
 - you use simple and clear language
 - your talk does not go over the time available
 - you will not need to read from your notes

Practice

1 Look at these expressions. In which part of a presentation would you expect them to be used?

1 Finally I'd like to remind you that we ...
2 If you have any questions I'll be happy to answer them at the end.
3 On this next slide you can see how our results have improved ...
4 Before I start my talk I'd just like to thank ...
5 This brings me to the next point ...
6 I'll discuss each point briefly and then give you my recommendations.
7 I hope you have found my comments useful and ...
8 This chart gives a comparison of potential returns on investment ...

2 Work in groups. Group A turn to page 145. Group B turn to page 137. Use the information to prepare a three-minute presentation on each company. Practise your presentation. Then make your presentation to the other group.

Culture at work

Attitudes to timing

Some cultures place a lot of importance on events starting and finishing on time. Others believe things should take as long as they need and are flexible with itineraries and schedules. What effect could this have on meetings, presentations and appointments? What is normal in your country?

Dilemma & Decision

Dilemma: Harley's Angels

Brief

Jeffrey Bleustein, CEO of Harley Davidson, was thinking about the future. He had already pulled the motorcycle manufacturer back from the brink of bankruptcy, but now he was thinking of the serious problems that lay ahead. And top of the list was the fact that Harley Davidson customers were definitely ageing. The black leather Angels were getting greyer every day. From an average age of 36 ten years ago the customer was now edging closer to 46. But what to do? Bleustein decided that he would put the question to his team of advisors at the next meeting of the strategic leadership council. In fact, maybe he'd better tell them what he wanted them to do right now – that way at the meeting they could present their ideas directly. Bleustein reached for the phone.

Task 1

Work in groups. Prepare a proposal for the leadership council. Decide whether your approach should be marketing, product, acquisition or distribution based. Turn to page 143 for some suggested ideas.

Company and market information on Harley Davidson/Buell

Market share	US	25%
	Europe	7%
Income sources	Motorcycles	80%
	Accessories, parts, clothing	20%
Demographics	91% of purchasers are male	
Average age	46 years old	
Average income	$79,000	

Task 2

Prepare a three-minute presentation to the council. Write a structure for your presentation and make notes under key headings. Then write an introduction and conclusion. Remember to include any helpful visual aids and stress your action points.

Task 3

Practise your presentation until it sounds natural and lasts three minutes. Make any necessary changes. Then present your proposal to the rest of the class.

Write it up

Write a formal memo to Jeffrey Bleustein outlining your proposal and its recommendations. (See Style guide, page 22.)

Useful phrases

I'd like to start by ...

I'll discuss ...

This brings me to the next point ...

This chart gives a ...

Finally, I'd like to ...

Decision:

- Listen to Laurence Bayerling, professor of management, explaining how Harley Davidson approached this dilemma.

Review 1

Language check

Present simple and continuous

Complete the sentences with the appropriate form of the present simple or continuous.

1 She is the director of a company which (manufacture) _____ biotech drugs.

2 Her day (start) _____ at 8 am.

3 She usually (not / finish) _____ until late in the evening.

4 Right now the company (look) _____ for a new CEO.

5 It (take) _____ longer than they thought it would.

6 They (know) _____ that choosing the right person is critical.

7 The company (go) _____ through a difficult time at the moment.

8 We (not / move) _____ into our new offices until next year.

Articles

Complete the text with either a definite or indefinite article or no article at all (ø).

> 1 _____ 'Learn to Lead' seminar and workshop provides 2 _____ senior management staff with 3 _____ excellent opportunity to learn and apply 4 _____ very latest leadership techniques: techniques that have been developed and tested in 5 _____ wide variety of challenging business environments and which have yielded 6 _____ exciting insights into business leadership.

Future forms

Complete the sentences with an appropriate future form.

1 The press launch (take) _____ place at 9:30 on Friday morning.

2 I've tried reconnecting the computer but I'm afraid it just (not / work) _____ .

3 Jane has just told me that she (leave) _____ the company.

4 Can I help you with that? I (sort) _____ it out in no time.

5 We (have) _____ lunch at the Thai restaurant. Why don't you join us?

6 I don't care whose fault it is. I just want to know what you (do) _____ about it.

7 We (launch) _____ the new corporate identity on 27 May.

8 Leave it with us. We (get) _____ back to you as soon as we can.

Consolidation

Underline the correct forms of the words in *italics*.

PHILIPS

Philips, with almost $30bn in annual sales, is one of [1] *ø / the* Europe's biggest corporations. It not only [2] *is producing / produces* billions of light bulbs and lamps every year but it also [3] *is supplying / supplies* TV tubes to almost 20 per cent of [4] *ø / the* world's TV manufacturers. But there is one thing the Philips consumer products group [5] *isn't doing / doesn't do*: and that's make [6] *a / the* profit. Gerard Kleisterlee, the newly appointed CEO, is about to change all that. Kleisterlee has introduced [7] *the / a* series of changes to streamline the way the company operates; centralising business processes, selling off unprofitable subsidiaries and focusing research on [8] *ø / the* innovative new products. In the USA he [9] *delivers / is delivering* an ultimatum: either its consumer division [10] *starts / is starting* to make money or it [11] *will / is going* to have to be closed. In Europe Philips [12] *builds / is building* a new hi-tech HQ, which it hopes [13] *is going to / will* facilitate flexibility and networking. All of this will be essential if the company [14] *is going to / will* produce the results that its shareholders expect. But Kleisterlee is optimistic; he believes his vision of Philip's future [15] *will / is going to* guide the company back to profitability.

Vocabulary check

1 Put the words in the correct groups.

forecasts   delegate   entrepreneur   subordinate
threat   shareholder   authority   producer
hierarchy   supervise   growth   planning
opportunity   task   subsidiary

companies	leadership	strategy

2 Now use the words to complete the text.

Viviane Rowland is the managing director of a
small company, Tristar Laminates, which she
founded with a group of fellow [1] _____ in
June 2000. Together they had successfully
identified a business [2] _____ to produce
fibreglass components for the marine industry.
Initially the three founders were the only
[3] _____ in the company but it soon became
clear that they would need extra capital. They
eventually managed to convince a local
businessman to invest £50,000 in exchange for
30 per cent of the company. Since then Tristar's
[4] _____ has been spectacular and Viviane
now [5] _____ a staff of 18 people and an
operation with half a million pounds in sales.
[6] _____ for the future is the immediate
problem that the company has to face. At the
moment production is carried out in a factory
that has become too small but finding an
alternative site is not an easy [7] _____ . 'This
industry is a dangerous one for small
[8] _____ like ourselves who only have
limited resources,' Viviane says, 'and when we
make a strategic decision like this we can't afford
to get it wrong.'

Career skills

Talking about your job

Match the sentence halves.

1   She reports to ...
2   I'm responsible for ...
3   My job involves ...
4   I work for ...

a   a team of five software developers.
b   a lot of planning and negotiating.
c   a small consulting firm.
d   the director of human resources.

Getting things done

Put the dialogue in the correct order.

☐ a   I'm really getting behind with that new
       proposal. I'll never get it done on time.

☐ a   I've got too many other things to do. I
       don't suppose you could give me a hand
       with it?

☐ a   It'd be great if you could have a look at
       the prices and check my figures.

☐ b   That's fine. I'll do that today. Anything
       else?

☐ b   Sure, what exactly can I do to help?

☐ b   Is that the one for the Spanish office?
       What seems to be the problem?

Short presentations

Match the sentence halves.

1   Finally I'd just like to say ...
2   On this next slide ...
3   I'll discuss ...
4   That brings me ...

a   you'll see how this has affected our
    performance.
b   each of these points in more detail later.
c   to the last part of this talk.
d   how much I've enjoyed making this
    presentation.

Unit 4
Pay

www.longman-elt.com   www.economist.com

Because I'm worth it

Keynotes

CEOs and top senior executives are sometimes referred to as '**fat cats**' because of the enormous **pay packages** and **rewards** they are offered when joining a company. These may include details of salary, **pension** and, frequently, even the possibility of a '**golden parachute**' or very generous **severance deal**, which is the sum of money they are guaranteed when they leave the company. Pay deals are negotiated by **remuneration committees** (**compensation committees** in the US) and are voted on by shareholders.

The new millionaires

Silicon Valley, San Francisco's capital of the hi-tech industry, produces dozens of new millionaires every day. Listen to two of them talk about life and complete the table below.

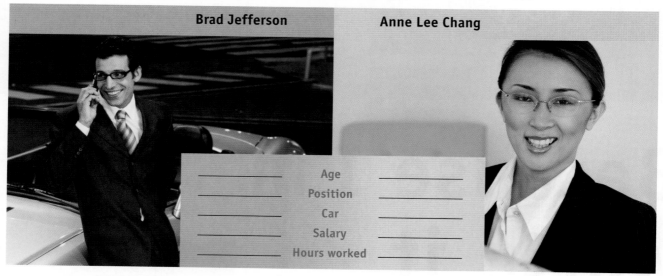

Brad Jefferson		Anne Lee Chang
_____	Age	_____
_____	Position	_____
_____	Car	_____
_____	Salary	_____
_____	Hours worked	_____

Speaking **Do you think anyone should earn so much money? Why? / Why not?**

Reading ## Executive pay

1 Read the text on the opposite page about bosses who perform badly but earn huge salaries. Do you think all pay should be based on performance?

2 Read the text again and choose the best answer for each question.

1 Who refused to approve GSK's remuneration committee's report?
   a   the board of directors
   b   the shareholders
   c   the chief executive

2 The company is now in a difficult position because
   a   it had already agreed to the new pay packages.
   b   it has to decide whether to approve the report or not.
   c   Jean-Pierre Garnier will take legal action.

3 What annoyed shareholders most about Garnier's pay package?
   a   It didn't reward his performance.
   b   His annual salary was too high.
   c   There was no link to performance.

4 Badly performing executives are sometimes paid large sums to
   a   encourage them to perform better.
   b   persuade them to leave the company.
   c   stop them from going to competitors.

5 The change in public mood will mean that in future
   a   salaries for chief executives will be lower.
   b   it will be harder to recruit chief executives.
   c   all executive pay will be linked to performance.

Executive pay

The rewards of failure

The trouble with the GlaxoSmithKline pay package was its reward for failure

When the public mood changes, the realisation can take time to sink in. Behaviour that was once acceptable can overnight come to be seen as outrageous. The board of GlaxoSmithKline, a big pharmaceutical company, has found itself at the sharp end of such a mood change. Its shareholders voted to reject the company's remuneration committee report, which would have paid Jean-Pierre Garnier, its Chief Executive, $35m if he lost his job and treated him and his wife as three years older than they actually are for the purpose of increasing their pensions.

The vote is purely advisory, with no binding force. But it leaves the company in a sort of legal limbo. More importantly, it leaves boardrooms everywhere in a difficult position. The message of shareholder discontent with large executive pay packages and poor corporate performance has never been so clear.

Company bosses have been slow to understand the new mood of outrage among shareholders. Shareholders have for years accepted that "fat cat" bosses paid themselves more or less whatever they liked. So it is uncomfortable to face criticism. But behind the criticism is a strong feeling that many chief executives are living according to quite a different set of rules from everyone else.

Although the value of most large companies has fallen considerably over the last few years, bosses have continued to pay themselves more. The value of their pensions has increased and they have struck lavish deals in the form of "golden parachute" severance deals to cushion their fall if they leave. Some of the aspects of Mr Garnier's package that most irritated the shareholders were ones that appeared to reward not superior performance but simply being there. Lots of bosses have such components in their pay.

Of course, companies may set up deals with bosses they no longer want in order to encourage them to go quickly and without a legal fight. But a generous advance promise to reward failure is no way to encourage success. Like the "guaranteed bonus" and the lifetime free dental treatment, it offers chief executives a one-way bet.

If the GSK vote makes companies cautious about such deals, that is welcome. The market for chief executives is far from perfect. There is no rate for the job, positions are often quietly filled rather than openly advertised and boardroom search committees rarely ask, "Could we get someone equally good even if we paid a bit less?" If the board now has to defend its compensation decisions publicly, it may be easier to say "We'd love to give you a golden parachute but the shareholders would make a fuss." More fuss, please, from shareholders. It's their company, after all ■

Speaking **How much say should shareholders have in executive pay deals?**

Replace the *italicised* words below with words and phrases from the box.

| pension | reject | criticism | advise | compensation | legal action |
| bonus | make a fuss |

1 Large companies are not used to *disapproval* from shareholders.

2 Our senior managers receive a *one-off payment* if they meet their targets.

3 The shareholders *don't accept* the remuneration committee's findings.

4 The CEO lost his *court case* demanding compensation after the board of directors asked him to leave.

5 The consultants *recommend* the company not to increase the CEO's pay.

6 The new CEO negotiated a lavish *retirement package*.

7 The *remuneration* committee decided not to offer a 'golden hello'.

8 The newspapers always *cause outrage* when large companies make their executive pay deals public.

Multi-part verbs

Study these multi-part verbs taken from the text.

Type 1: **without an object**

*When the public mood changes, the realisation can take time to **sink in**.*

Type 2: **with an object**

*Of course, companies may **set up deals** with bosses they no longer want in order to encourage them to go quickly and without a legal fight.*

Complete the sentences with the correct form of multi-part verbs from the box. Which verbs need an object?

| point out | set up | look after | call on | buy up | step down |
| get ahead | go under | break down | call off |

1 If we hadn't _*bought up*_ so many companies we wouldn't be so short of cash. *(type 2)*

2 The shareholders feel that he should really _____ because of the mess the finances are in.

3 We had to _____ the meeting because the export manager missed his plane.

4 Our sales executive will _____ you next week to show you our new range of products.

5 Could you please _____ the new recruit, she doesn't know where anything is.

6 Negotiations _____ after an hour because they just couldn't find a compromise.

7 If turnover is as low as last year we'll probably _____.

8 The only way to _____ in this company is to work harder than anyone else.

9 We finally _____ a subsidiary in Spain last year.

10 As she _____ in her presentation, competition is rising and prices are falling.

Listening 1 **1 Listen to a financial analyst talk about salaries and share options. Listen to part one and complete the information below.**

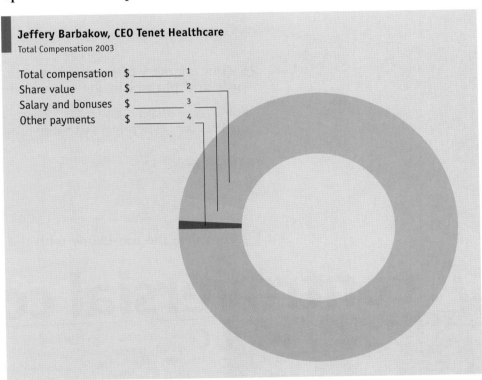

Jeffery Barbakow, CEO Tenet Healthcare
Total Compensation 2003

Total compensation $ _____ 1
Share value $ _____ 2
Salary and bonuses $ _____ 3
Other payments $ _____ 4

2 In part two she talks about evaluating and rewarding performance. Listen and answer the questions.

1 What were stock options intended to do?

2 How can market changes affect stock options?

3 How do some managers exploit this situation?

4 How are employees generally evaluated?

5 Would this work for managers?

6 How can we measure CEO performance?

Speaking **Work in pairs. Student A turn to page 138. Student B turn to page 140. Ask and answer questions to complete the information about CEOs awarded large severance deals after ruining companies.**

Present perfect and past simple

Study the examples of the present perfect and past tenses taken from the text on page 35 and answer the questions below.

a   *Company bosses **have been** slow to understand the new mood of outrage among shareholders.*

b   *... a big pharmaceutical company, **has found** itself at the sharp end of such a mood change.*

c   *... poor corporate performance **has never been** so clear.*

d   *Its shareholders voted to reject the company's remuneration committee report ....*

1   Which sentences refer to recent or unfinished time? Which tense is used?

2   Which sentence refers to finished time? Which tense is used?

For more information, see page 158.

1 Time markers often decide which tense to use. Put the following words and phrases in the correct groups below.

| ago | this | never | yesterday | ever | the last few | since | in 2005 |
| on Tuesday | recently | last week | today | yet | already | for | 8 April |

finished time	recent / unfinished time

2 Complete the text below with the appropriate tense of the verbs.

A controversial court case

Cantor Fitzgerald (¹be) *has been* tragically famous since September 11th 2001, when it (²lose)_____ 658 of its staff in the World Trade Center. Recently, it (³appear)_____ back in the news in Britain because one of its staff (⁴take)_____ it to court for breach of contract. Steven Honkulak (⁵be)_____ the managing director of interest rates derivatives, which is a highly stressful job but he (⁶earn)_____ £400,000 plus bonuses.

However, his boss, Lee Amaitis, who (⁷work)_____ with the company for many years is a very tough and aggressive man. Mr Honkulak claims that Mr Amaitis, regularly (⁸threaten)_____ to dismiss him and (⁹cause)_____ him so much stress that he (¹⁰start)_____ to drink and take medication. He finally (¹¹leave)_____ the company and (¹²ask)_____ for £1m compensation. The company defended itself by saying 'Mr Amaitis (¹³contribute)_____ to the success of this company with his vision and hard work. Mr Honkulak, however (¹⁴want)_____ the rewards of the senior position but his weaknesses made him unable to cope with the job.' The judge awarded Mr Honkulak £1m, saying that there are limits beyond which no employer should go.

1 Do you think Mr Honkulak deserved to receive £1m compensation? Why? / Why not?

2 Work in pairs. What recent events and developments have there been in your country? Think about the following.

• politics   • the economy   • celebrity life   • sport   • fashion

Evaluating performance

Performance is usually evaluated by looking at past objectives and deciding whether they have been met. If they have not been met, the person being evaluated can give reasons why and new objectives can be fixed. Below are some expressions you might hear during an evaluation session.

We had real problems with ...
There's been a slight overspend on the ...
We were behind schedule but we managed to catch up.
We've come in under budget.
It hasn't been easy but we managed to hit our deadline in the end.
The deadline's too tight. We're not going to meet it.

Listening 2 ⊙

A project manager and one of his team evaluate the progress of a project. Put the dialogue in the correct order. Then listen and check your answer.

A ☐ That might be difficult. What's the problem?

A ☐ Well, I can maybe negotiate a two-day extension. Leave it with me, I'll see what I can do. Will you still come in on budget?

A ☐ How's it going with the Titanium project? Are you going to be able to meet the deadline?

B ☐ We've had real technical problems. The whole network shut down last week for two days.

B ☐ Possibly. We were behind schedule last month. We've almost caught up but the deadline's still too tight. Could we extend it?

B ☐ Not now. The network problems have meant we've had to contract a lot of the work out to meet the deadline, so there'll be an overspend on the data processing. It shouldn't be too much though.

Speaking

Work in pairs. Find out about a recent deadline your partner had to meet. Did they meet it? If so, what helped them meet it? If not, what went wrong and what lesson did they learn from it?

Culture at work

Fixed objectives or flexibility?

Objectives-focused cultures clearly define objectives and detail roles and tasks in writing. Flexible cultures build relationships first and let goals develop with the relationship. What is common in your culture? How might this difference cause misunderstanding in multicultural teams?

Dilemma & Decision

Dilemma: Success at what price?

Brief

Better Prices, a large UK supermarket chain, is in financial difficulties. The departing CEO, Mark Crawley, had promised that dramatic transformations would lead to higher returns and rising share price. However, he began by signing a disastrous merger deal and since then the share value has halved! In spite of this, he awarded himself several bonuses on top of his £790,000 a year salary and leaves with a golden parachute worth over £2m. The outraged shareholders have decided to work closely with the board in choosing his successor from the following short list of candidates.

Marjorie Sweetman, successful CEO of a chain of department stores that was losing money when she took over five years ago. She believes in people and steady progress. She would cut growth targets by half. She hasn't asked for a golden parachute and would agree to bonuses linked to performance. She does, however, expect generous share options and a salary of £650,000. Her strategy will mean a short-term fall in dividends.

John Creed, currently MD of a company famous for training Europe's top managers. If recruited, the share price would shoot up in the short-term. He is the most expensive candidate at £750,000 p.a. He wants a contract for a minimum of ten years and a guaranteed $2.4m pension deal not linked to performance. He believes he can succeed in 100 days and plans dramatic changes in policy and staff.

David Preston, current Chief Operating Officer. His pay is £650,000 plus bonuses and share options. He would expect a big salary increase but proposes, however, not to replace himself as COO and do both jobs. He argues newcomers lack the knowledge of the company and its staff. He wants a generous pension when he leaves and plans to increase shareholder dividends at once.

Task 1

Work in groups. You are the shareholders. Look at the candidates and discuss the advantages and disadvantages of each in terms of pay and potential performance.

Task 2

Prepare to present your ideas to the class and make a final recommendation.

Task 3

Present the arguments for your chosen candidate to the class.

Write it up

Write a formal memo to the board comparing the candidates and making a final recommendation. (See Style guide, page 22.)

Decision:

⊙ Listen to Liam Mellows, a retired remuneration committee and board member of another well known retailing company, talking about which candidate *he* thinks the board should recommend to the shareholders.

> **Useful phrases**
>
> ... has never ...
> ... has worked here for ...
> ... hasn't tried to ...
> ... has promised to ...

Unit 5 Development

www.longman-elt.com   www.economist.com

Prosperity or preservation?

Keynotes

Economic development has brought **benefits** to the populations of both the **more** and the **less economically developed countries** (**MEDC** and **LEDC**). Loans from international organisations enable governments to exploit their **natural resources** and to invest in **construction projects** and **industrial facilities**. This raises **Gross Domestic Product** (**GDP**) and improves standards of living. **Environmentalists** oppose development which produces **pollution** and **endangers** the health of local people and depletes resources.

Economic development

How has the quality of life changed in your country over the last few years? What do young people have today that their parents didn't have?

Kristen Neymarc is an analyst at the OECD (Organisation of Economic Cooperation and Development). Listen to her explain what the OECD does and answer the questions.

1 What are the origins of the OECD?
2 What sort of work does it do?
3 How is the OECD changing?

Development and the environment

1 Read the article on the opposite page about a proposed development project in the Peruvian rainforest. Are the following organisations for or against the project? What are their reasons?

Organisation	For / Against	Reason
Peruvian government.............		
Pluspetrol		
Amazon Watch.................		
Inter-American Development Bank		
US Import-Export Bank		

2 Read the article again. Which of the following will happen if the Camisea project goes ahead?

1 Peru will again become an exporter of fuel.
2 The IDB loan could release further finance for the scheme.
3 The Peruvian government will be able to give financial assistance to some of the poorer areas in the country.
4 Peruvian companies will be able to reduce some of their costs.
5 A road will be built through the Peruvian jungle.
6 The project will stop without the loans.

3 According to its opponents, the Camisea project will have a negative impact in a number of areas. List four things that they say will be affected.

What do you think will happen to the Camisea project? Why?

Glossary

upstream supply of items for production

downstream supply of finished products to consumers

GDP a country's annual productivity

greens environmentalists

consortium group of companies

Development and the environment

Gas for Peru v green imperialism

LIMA

Where should the balance between development and the environment be struck? And who should strike it?

AFTER nearly two decades of contract negotiations, natural gas from the Amazon jungle looks finally set to reach Peru's capital, Lima, by next August. However, US environmentalists are making a final attempt to stop the $1.5 billion project, which if it goes ahead should turn Peru from an importer of fuel into an exporter.

Camisea has huge gas reserves, more than enough to supply Lima for many years. In 2000, Peru's government awarded a licence to develop the field to an "upstream" consortium headed by Pluspetrol of Argentina and Hunt Oil, a US firm. A second "downstream" consortium is building a 700km pipeline to the coast. There will also be two plants on the Pacific coast to process and export gas to Mexico and energy-hungry California.

But the lobbying, led by Amazon Watch, caused the Inter-American Development Bank (IDB) last week to put off a decision on a $75m loan for the pipeline. Approval by the IDB might unlock another loan, of $200m, for the "upstream" consortium, from the United States Export-Import Bank.

Unfortunately, Camisea itself is deep in the Peruvian jungle. Its opponents claim that the project threatens tribes of Amazon Indians, rare species and the rainforest along the pipeline route and that the export terminals would endanger a marine reserve at Paracas. Certainly, some Indians died from disease after first coming in contact with workers in the mid-1980s. But Camisea's defenders argue that its benefits are huge and that any social and environmental costs can be minimised.

Peru, once an oil exporter, now imports some $500m of fuel a year. Camisea is going to provide cleaner, cheaper energy for local consumers, as well as exports. The IDB estimates that the project would add 0.8 per cent a year to Peru's GDP over its 30-year life. Jaime Quijandría, the economy minister, says that it should generate tax revenues of up to $200m a year, much of which will go to the poorest areas through which the pipeline passes.

Lobbying by the greens has forced the government and the developers to take precautions. The consortium is using "offshore" technology at Camisea – drilling sites are being operated as if they were islands in the jungle. Workers and supplies are helicoptered in. There are no access roads. Jungle will soon cover over the scars left by construction work.

None of this satisfies the more radical US greens, such as Amazon Watch. They claim massive soil damage is taking place along the pipeline. They also oppose the planned location of the export terminals. These are close to the Paracas marine but in an area already damaged by industry.

Without the loans, Camisea may still go ahead. But the project would take longer and might finish up having less money to spend on protecting the environment. Some of the concerns about Camisea's environmental and social risks are no doubt real. Bodies such as the IDB can help. But many Peruvians think it should be for Peru to decide whether and how to make best use of its natural resources.■

Word form

1 Some words in English can be used as both nouns and verbs. Look at the examples below. Read the definitions for the following words from the text. Which of the two definitions was used?

1	contract (line 1)	(n) written legal agreement
		(v) give work to a supplier
2	project (line 7)	(n) planned piece of work
		(v) calculate the cost of something
3	fuel (line 44)	(n) substance burned for energy
		(v) make a bad situation worse
4	plant (line 18)	(n) industrial complex
		(v) put something into the ground
5	process (line 19)	(n) series of actions
		(v) treat or modify a substance
6	loan (line 25)	(n) financial assistance
		(v) give something on a temporary basis

2 Are the noun forms and verb forms pronounced in the same way? Which ones are different?

3 Complete the sentences with the correct form of the following words.

plant   concern   benefit   estimate   test   award

1   The principal _____ for the area will be higher employment.
2   It is impossible to _____ the real value of the rainforest.
3   The government will _____ the contract to a foreign consortium.
4   A series of _____ will be conducted to measure pollution levels.
5   Construction of both the new _____ will be completed next year.
6   This is an issue that _____ everybody.

Development and the environment

Put the words and phrases in the correct groups. Use a dictionary to help you.

access roads   jungle   drilling sites   reserves   tribes   terminals
gas field   plants   rainforest   pipeline   rare species

Construction	Environment
access roads	*jungle*

Modal verbs of likelihood

Look at the following sentences. Do they express certainty, probability or possibility?

1 Camisea *is going to mean* cheaper fuel for local people.
2 Camisea *will add* 0.8 per cent a year to Peru's GDP.
3 Approval by the IDB *might unlock* another loan of $200m.
4 Without the loans, Camisea *may still go* ahead.
5 The export terminals *would endanger* a marine reserve.
6 ... it *should generate* tax revenues of up to $200m a year.
7 The survey *must be* very positive for the company to invest so much.

For more information, see page 159.

1 Choose the appropriate modal forms to complete the following statements about the Brazilian rainforest.

1 According to some calculations 16 per cent of the forest area ___*may*___ already have been destroyed.
  a may   b will   c would

2 Greenpeace have suggested that it _____ be possible to reduce deforestation if traditional forms of agriculture are promoted.
  a is going to   b might   c must

3 Many plant species are currently being studied in the hope that they _____ provide sources for new drugs.
  a should   b would   c will

4 Some international organisations are campaigning for the extension of reserves. This _____ safeguard 30 per cent of the forest from industry.
  a must   b might   c would

5 Some experts point out that many forestry workers live from day to day and that they _____ do anything to obtain enough money to eat.
  a should   b must   c will

6 Logging companies pay as little as $15 to buy trees that _____ be worth several thousand if they were sold on the international markets.
  a could   b will   c can

7 Some landowners are not concerned about the law because they know that they _____ have to pay the fines that are sometimes imposed.
  a won't   b mightn't   c shouldn't

2 Complete the extract from a presentation about the future of the world's natural energy reserves with the following modal verbs. More than one answer is often possible.

will   may   might   would   should   could

Thank you for inviting me here today to make this presentation about the future of our natural energy reserves. I know some of you ¹ ___will___ already be familiar with the complex nature of this subject and I hope you ² _____ forgive me for trying to deal with it in only 45 minutes.

If we look back to twenty years ago I can recall how confident people were that nuclear energy ³ _____ provide the ultimate energy source and I don't think that anyone at that time ⁴ _____ possibly imagine the impact that the accident at Chernobyl ⁵ _____ have on our confidence in that industry. While the nuclear industry ⁶ _____ still hold out some hope for a nuclear-powered future – this time in the form of nuclear fusion – it now looks like it ⁷ _____ be some time before the necessary technologies are in place for it to succeed. Indeed some sceptics ⁸ _____ even go as far as to say that ⁹ _____never be the case! So from a world of confidence we now face the uncomfortable facts: fossil fuels are finite resources and while they ¹⁰ _____ be sufficient to carry our economies through the next few decades, there is no doubt that beyond that horizon new sources of energy ¹¹ _____ have to be developed in order to sustain our current economic model.

Speaking

1 Look at some of the major changes predicted for the future. When do you think they are most likely to happen?

1 Cloned human organs are available.
2 Sea levels rise, causing mass flooding.
3 Life is found on another planet.
4 Space travel is freely available.
5 Electronic money replaces cash completely.
6 Cars are banned from city centres.
7 Super viruses create chaos across the world's computers.
8 One currency is introduced for all countries.

2 Prepare a short presentation of how you see your own future career. Include information about what you would like to happen and how you think your life will change in the coming years.

Showing cause and effect

When talking about the consequences of events and situations it is useful to explain the reasons why we think something happened or will happen in the future. Look at the following examples.

*Building the terminal will **lead to** massive environmental damage.*
*The IDB put off the $75m loan **due to** lobbying by environmentalists.*
*A demonstration would **result in** lots of publicity.*
*Jobs will be created **as a result of** the inward investment.*
*The pollution was **caused by** a factory further up the river.*

 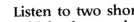

Listen to two short dialogues. What are the people talking about? Which phrases do they use to show cause and effect?

	subject	phrases
Extract 1		
Extract 2		

Read the following descriptions of possible scenarios. What do you think the consequences of each of these scenarios will / would be? Discuss your answers in pairs.

1   All the debt of developing countries is cancelled.
2   Global temperatures continue to rise.
3   Economically developed countries fail to reduce pollution levels.
4   Petroleum prices rise 500 per cent.
5   The cities of the world continue to attract more and more people.
6   The marine resources of the planet are not protected.

Dealing with unclear situations

Some cultures try to avoid unclear situations by use of fixed rules and procedures. Other cultures tolerate uncertainty and believe you need to be flexible to deal with problems as they arise. How might this affect business practices? Which attitude is more common in your country?

Dilemma & Decision

Dilemma: Striking a balance

Brief

You will be taking part in a discussion forum on the subject of the Camisea project at this year's Wild Earth conference. During the forum the various groups involved in the Camisea project will have an opportunity to present their different viewpoints. The following people will be present at the forum.

Group A • Consortium representatives (See page 144.)

Group B • Peruvian government representatives (See page 142.)

Group C • Amazon Watch (See page 138.)

Task 1

Work in groups. Choose one of the above roles and read the information at the back of the book.

Task 2

Prepare the arguments that your group will use to present at the forum. List the negative effects that the wrong course of action will have. Prepare to present your ideas to the class.

Task 3

In turn, each group makes a brief presentation of its view of the Camisea project.

Task 4

Once each group has presented, the class should try to agree if and how the Camisea project should continue.

Write it up

Write a short report outlining the key issues concerning the Camisea project and recommending the best course of action. (See Style guide, page 26.)

> **Useful phrases**
>
> the ... will mean ...
>
> ... will/could cause ...
>
> ... would endanger ...
>
> ... will/could lead to/result in ...
>
> ... would greatly benefit from ...
>
> ... may/might have a disastrous effect on ...

Decision:

⊙ Professor Harding is a development expert at the Darwin Institute in California. Listen to him talk about how complex projects like Camisea can be managed.

Unit 6
Marketing

www.longman-elt.com   www.economist.com

Seducing the masses

Keynotes

The various activities of the marketing process are referred to as the **marketing mix** and traditionally include the **four Ps: product** (characteristics and **features**), **price** (appropriate market price), **promotion** (communicating the product's **benefits**), **place** (**distribution** of the product in markets). In order to gain a **competitive advantage** over rivals, companies create **brands** that represent **aspirations** and a desirable image of life that the customer would like to identify with.

Brands

1 What are your favourite brands of the following products? Why do you prefer these to other similar brands?

soft drinks   clothes   cars   shampoo

2 Now choose one of the products you use and consider the marketing mix for that brand. Think about the following.

product – what are the product's features?

price – in comparison with similar products

promotion – where and how is it advertised?

place – where can you buy the product?

Do you think you are a typical customer for the brand?

3 People's attitudes to brands and marketing can be very different. Which of these statements do you agree with?

'Marketing transforms brands, making them stand for things that they just don't stand for. They don't deliver.' Naomi Klein author of No Logo: Taking Aim at the Brand Bullies.

'Brands provide us with beliefs. They define who we are.' Wally Olins, a corporate identity consultant.

Marketing brands

1 Read the text on the opposite page and decide which of the above views is closest to that of the author.

2 Read the text again and match the headings a–f with paragraphs 1–5. There is one extra heading.

a   Brands past   _____

b   Advertising brands   _____

c   The new consumers   _____

d   Guilty   _____

e   The case against brands _____

f   The importance of brands _____

3 Read paragraph three again. Are the statements true or false?

1   It was relatively easy in the past to create a new brand.

2   Buying a branded product did not cost customers more.

3   Brands were developed for the international market.

4   The government closely controlled the markets at home.

5   Brands deterred other companies from entering the market.

The author suggests young people no longer believe advertisements. Do you agree? What does influence young people's buying decisions?

Marketing brands

Money *can* buy you love

Glossary

manipulated influenced to do what someone else wants

corrupt make morally bad

aspirations hopes and wishes

bombarded repeatedly attacked

veterans very experienced people

Are we being manipulated into buying brands?

1 BRANDS are accused of all sorts of evils, from threatening our health and destroying our environment to corrupting our children. Brands are so powerful, it is said, that they force us to look alike, eat alike and be alike.

2 This grim picture has been made popular by many recent anti-branding books. The argument has been most forcefully stated in Naomi Klein's book *No Logo: Taking Aim at the Brand Bullies*. Its argument runs something like this. In the new global economy, brands represent a huge portion of the value of a company and, increasingly, its biggest source of profits. So companies are switching from showcasing product features to marketing aspirations and the dream of a more exciting lifestyle.

3 Historically, building a brand was rather simple. A logo was a straightforward guarantee of quality and consistency, or it was a signal that a product was something new. For that, consumers were prepared to pay a premium. Building a brand nationally required little more than an occasional advertisement on a handful of television or radio stations showing how the product tasted better or drove faster. There was little regulation. It was easy for brands such as Coca-Cola, Kodak and Marlboro to become hugely powerful. Because shopping was still a local business and competition limited, a successful brand could maintain its lead and high prices for years. A strong brand acted as an effective barrier to entry for competing products.

4 Consumers are now bombarded with choices. They are also harder to reach. They are busier, more distracted and have more media to choose from. They are "commercials veterans" experiencing up to 1,500 pitches a day. They are more cynical than ever about marketing and less responsive to messages to buy. Jonathan Bond and Richard Kirshenbaum, authors of *Under The Radar – Talking To Today's Cynical Consumers*, say "some of the most cynical consumers are the young." Nearly half of all US college students have taken marketing courses and "know the enemy". For them, "shooting down advertising has become a kind of sport.'"

5 Marketers have to take some of the blame. While consumers have changed beyond recognition, marketing has not. Even in the USA, home to nine of the world's ten most valuable brands, it can be a shockingly old-fashioned business. Marketing theory is still largely based on the days when Procter & Gamble's brands dominated the USA, and its advertising agencies wrote the rules. Those rules focused on the product and where to sell it, not the customer. The new marketing approach is to develop a brand not a product – to sell a lifestyle or a personality, to appeal to emotions. (It is a much harder task than describing the features and benefits of a product.) However, brands of the future will have to stand for all of this and more. Not only will they need to be a stamp of product quality and a promise of a more desirable lifestyle but they will also have to project an image of social responsibility ■

1 **Find words in the text on page 51 to complete the wordmap.**

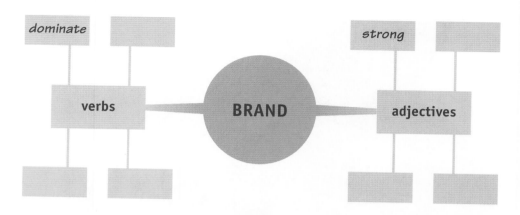

dominate

verbs

BRAND

strong

adjectives

2 **Complete the magazine article with the following words.**

cynical   consumers   competition   markets   effective   pitches
customers   marketers   impressed

Saying 'I do' to the marketers

When young couples get married in the USA they also receive a gift bag marked 'newly-wed kit'.

In a world of ever increasing
[1] *competition* many companies are happy to use this new way to reach
[2]_____ . Corporate
[3]_____ say that certain points in life make people especially vulnerable to sales [4]_____ . Companies such as Procter & Gamble have found this to be a very [5]_____ way to target extremely profitable
[6]_____ such as young couples. US newly-weds spend an average of $70bn in the first year of marriage. One study shows that 67 per cent of women wear the same perfume they wore when they got married and a Bride's magazine study showed that after three years of marriage women were still [7]_____ of the same stores they had shopped in before the wedding. While the gift bags do appeal to a lot of young couples, others are a little less [8]_____ . As one rather [9]_____ young man said when he found a sample of deodorant and an offer for a new chequebook in his gift bag, 'does this mean that marriage stands for body odour and financial worries? This stuff seems better suited for a divorce kit!'

Speaking   **What do you think about this method of marketing? Can you think of other 'points in life' when people would be 'particularly vulnerable' to marketing tactics such as these?**

Comparatives and superlatives

Look at the following sentences from the text on page 51.

1 *They are also harder to reach. They are busier, more distracted and have more media to choose from.*

2 *In the new global economy, brands represent a huge portion of the value of a company and, increasingly, its biggest source of profits.*

3 *Jonathan Bond and Richard Kirshenbaum, authors of* Under The Radar – Talking To Today's Cynical Consumers, *say 'some of the most cynical consumers are the young.'*

4 *The argument has been most forcefully stated in Naomi Klein's book* No Logo: Taking Aim at the Brand Bullies.

How are the comparatives and superlatives of the following formed?

– adjectives of one syllable
– adjectives ending in -y?
– adjectives of more than one syllable
– adverbs

 For more information, see page 159.

Practice   **1 Complete the table.**

	adjective	comparative	superlative	adverb	comparative	superlative
1	powerful	more powerful	most powerful	powerfully	more powerfully	most powerfully
2	exciting					
3	fast					
4	cynical					
5	easy					
6	hard					
7	responsive					
8	good					

The only thing to worry about in this vehicle is low flying aircraft

2 **Complete the article with the correct form of the adjectives in brackets.**

That little voice in your head

Laser-like audio technology is currently being developed to provide marketers with one of the (¹new) _newest_ and (²innovative)_____ marketing techniques they've seen for years. Hypersonic sound speakers on supermarket shelves and vending machines send messages to customers as they walk past. The sound is (³clear)_____ than normal, which allows it to reach directly into the listeners' ears. They will think the message is coming from inside their heads! Marketers believe that it will have a far (⁴great)_____ effect on sales than other forms of point of sale promotion. 'It will also make people laugh,' one consultant said, 'it is (⁵funny)_____ and (⁶amusing)_____ way to sell

that I've ever heard of.' But some people are (⁷sceptical)_____ about consumer reaction. People may not like the fact that this method is (⁸intrusive)_____ than others. But marketers remain optimistic as one consultant said, 'This is (⁹good)_____ chance we've got of ever actually getting inside our customers' heads.'

Listening 1 ⊙ **The importance of brands**

1 **Pat Hill is a brand strategy consultant. Listen to her talk about the importance of brands and answer the questions.**

1   Why do companies need to create brands?
2   What are the five most important characteristics of a brand?

_____   _____

_____   _____

_____

3   Why has Chanel No 5 been successful for so long?
4   What helped establish the No 5 brand in the 1960s?

Speaking   **2** **Can you think of other celebrity endorsements?**

A successful brand appeals to people's emotions and desires. Match the following slogans to the types of appeal.

1   Don't leave home without it   a   patriotism
2   Think Different   b   self-esteem
3   It keeps going and going and going c   insecurity
4   Because I'm worth it   d   originality
5   The great American chocolate   e   value for money

Considering alternatives

When considering alternatives it is important to show the degree of difference between them. By using quantifiers we can show our preferences and argue for them more persuasively.

The new design will cost slightly more but look a lot better.

Listening 2 ☉ Listen to eight short extracts where people express to what degree they prefer certain alternatives. Complete the table below with the quantifiers you hear.

Minor difference	Major difference
slightly	*much*
a bit	
a little / a few	

Can you think of others to add to the table?

Speaking Which of these cars would you choose to buy? Compare them in terms of price, style, reliability, image, etc.

Factual or vague?

Some cultures believe that all statements should be honest, accurate, unemotional and not open to interpretation. Other cultures prefer to modify statements with understatement (*somewhat, slightly*) and exaggeration or even leave the true meaning unsaid. What is common in your country? How might this difference cause misunderstanding in multicultural teams?

Dilemma & Decision

Dilemma: A scent of risk

Brief

Bellissima is an Italian perfume and cosmetics business. The company has a highly successful range of products in the luxury cosmetics market. It is planning to launch a new fragrance and extensive market research has produced detailed profiles of two potential target markets as described below. Bellissima now has to decide whether to expand its current market base or risk branching out and reaching a new client.

Profile A

High-income women aged 25–30, who spend a high proportion of income on restaurants and theatre. Currently loyal to our cosmetics range but change perfume brands from time to time. However, they already have a positive image of our brand so a relatively limited promotional campaign would be enough to create an awareness of the new product. They accept high prices for quality products.

Packaging should be simple but elegant, using expensive materials in dark colours. The brand should appeal to a sense of ambition and superiority. Suggested brand names: *Sophistication* or *Cool Elegance*.

Profile B

Women aged 18–25, who like popular music, clothes, going out and don't mind paying high prices for quality or products that are 'in fashion'. Currently don't use our brands as consider them slightly old fashioned. We would need to spend a lot on promotion to attract this target who are not high earners but spend a high proportion of income on clothes and cosmetics.

Packaging to represent a young, carefree lifestyle with a strong and rebellious personality. Regular packaging updates needed to keep up with fashion trends. Suggested brand names: *Rebel Angel* or *She Devil*.

Task 1

Work in groups. Discuss the advantages of each profile and decide which option has most potential for Bellissima.

Task 2

Now choose a brand name and plan your brand strategy. Consider the four Ps of the marketing mix.

Task 3

Present your concept and brand strategy to the class.

Write it up

Write an action plan for the Marketing Director at Bellissima with a summary of your group's strategy. (See Style guide, page 24.)

Decision:

- Rosemary Weinberger, is a brand consultant at Scott & Ridley Associates. Listen to her discuss the dilemma and find out which option she would choose.

> **Useful phrases**
>
> ... is a bit / slightly more ...
> ... is by far the better alternative
> ... is a lot / way too ...
> ... is the best / most ...

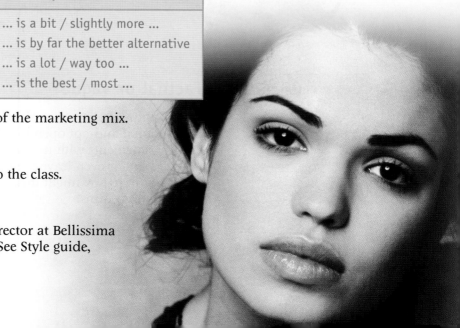

Review 2

Language check

Present perfect and past simple

Complete the text with the appropriate past forms of the verbs in brackets.

The Ford Motor Company, which (¹be)_____ in business for over 100 years, (²reach)_____ a critical moment in its history. Dwindling market share, a saturated domestic market and falling prices are just some of the problems that William Clay Ford Jr, the new CEO, (³have) _____ to face since he (⁴take over) _____ the top job in 2001. The company (⁵perform) _____ poorly in recent years. The latest figures indicate that Ford's share of the European market (⁶fall) _____ by as much as four per cent. In the USA the situation is little better. Nissan (⁷open) _____ a new factory in 2003 and last year (⁸produce) _____ 400,000 pick-ups and sports utility vehicles (SUVs), which are exactly the sort of vehicles that the Ford Motor Company (⁹rely on) _____ over the years to provide its profit. But William Clay Ford Jr is fighting back. He (¹⁰shift) _____ the company's focus away from luxury brands like Aston Martin and Jaguar and back to the less glamorous but more profitable vehicles such as the F-150, the best selling pick-up in the USA.

Modal verbs of likelihood

Underline any inappropriate modal verbs in the following sentences. Then correct them.

1   Estimates of the pollution in the area show that it would already be too late to save the wildlife.

2   Protection agencies have suggested that it must be possible to save some species if international funds can be found.

3   Negotiations are taking place between various organisations in the hope that they will come up with such funds.

4   I think they should publicise the full findings of the independent report.

5   Might you read the report and give your opinion?

6   Water pollution really might be stopped soon if we want to protect the wildlife on the lake.

Comparatives and superlatives

Comparatives and superlatives

Read the text and correct any mistakes in the *italicised* comparative and superlative forms.

The ¹ *later* report from the Executive Watch Foundation shows that executive pay is becoming the ² *biggest* worry of corporate governance – even ³ *most* worrying than the question of the independence of auditors. In the USA the SEC is already proposing new and significantly ⁴ *tough* rules that are designed to make it ⁵ *more easily* for shareholders to nominate candidates to company boards. It is hoped that this will lead to ⁶ *greater* independence for directors and to ⁷ *lowest* remuneration packages for executives. Company directors and senior managers may also be about to receive far ⁸ *less* benefits such as stock options. The research has also shown that the companies that provided the ⁹ *greatest* number of stock options to executives were also those whose performance was the ¹⁰ *worse*.

Consolidation

Read the text and underline the correct forms of the words in *italics*.

In recent years the number of advertising messages ¹ *increased / has increased* to almost saturation point. Consumers ² *were / have been* easily influenced in the past but now they ³ *became / have become* ⁴ *more critical than / most critical than* before and ⁵ *have started / started* to analyse and question many marketing techniques.

As a result, marketers ⁶ *would / will* have to come up with more and more inventive ways to attract consumers. There ⁷ *was / has been* an increase in advertising to children recently, too. The current thinking is that as adults are considerably ⁸ *more cynical / most cynical* than children, it is ⁹ *better / best* to attract new customers to your brand when they are young – and that way they ¹⁰ *should / must* continue buying it all their lives – rather than trying to tempt customers away from other brands. This ¹¹ *may / must* not always be the case but it ¹² *might / will* usually lead to reflex buying of some brands. One thing is certain, marketers ¹³ *will / may* continue to find ¹⁴ *newest / new* ways to get consumers to part with their money.

Vocabulary check

1 Complete the text with the correct option A–C.

PR DISASTERS

Recent bad ¹_____ concerning many aspects of company policy has badly damaged the image and ²_____ we have built up over the years.

The first disaster struck when we were accused of using misleading ³_____ . Several groups of consumers claimed that our latest product did not perform as well as it should. Sales of our other ⁴_____ have also dropped as a result. One short-term solution is to trade the new product under a different name and ⁵_____ . The next problem concerns a group of environmentalists ⁶_____ against one of our manufacturing sites abroad. They are accusing us of using up local natural ⁷_____ .

To make matters worse, our CEO resigned over the affair and it became public that he had negotiated a very ⁸_____ severance deal on entering the company, including a huge ⁹_____ parachute. The ¹⁰_____ committee will have to explain to shareholders why they agreed to such a sum at a meeting next week.

1	A stories	B publicity	C news
2	A reputation	B trademark	C relations
3	A campaigning	B advertising	C selling
4	A marks	B names	C brands
5	A logo	B symbol	C sign
6	A disagreeing	B protesting	C complaining
7	A resources	B reserves	C reservations
8	A lavish	B superior	C fat
9	A golden	B safety	C goodbye
10	A remuneration	B salary	C pension

2 Use a verb and preposition from each list to replace the verbs in italics below.

verbs: step get set call look
prepositions: up after down ahead off

1 We *founded* the company in 1970.
2 They had to *cancel* the meeting because of the train strike.
3 My job is to *take care of* new recruits.
4 If you want to *get promoted* you have to work hard and believe in the company.
5 The CEO had to *leave* due to the financial scandal.

Career skills

Evaluating performance

Match the problem with the action taken.

1 The virus wiped out our accounting records.
2 The project was running very late.
3 It has probably never happened before.
4 Relationships in the team completely broke down.

a But we managed to resolve our differences.
b But we came in under budget!
c But we negotiated an extension on the deadline.
d Luckily we could get the data from backup files.

Predicting consequences

Complete the text with one of the following expressions of cause and effect.

caused by   due to   as a result of
resulted in   lead to

Experts are now suggesting that the record levels of deforestation in the Brazilian rainforest have occurred not ¹_____ traditional logging activities but rather because of a rise in the exports of beef. The increase in exports of beef and other commodities, which is at least partly ²_____ the recent devaluation of the Brazilian Real, has ³_____ a minor economic recovery in the country. However, it will also ⁴_____ greater pressure from farmers to clear forest land to make room for extra cows. How much more destruction of the forest will be ⁵_____ further clearance is now a subject of debate.

Considering alternatives

Read the following text. In some lines there is an incorrect extra word. Underline the incorrect word or write *correct* next to the line number.

1 This model is quite by far the most popular with
2 our customers. It has a little smaller engine so it is
3 slightly less powerful than as our standard model.
4 But on the other hand it is so far more economical.
5 It is also a little shorter in length, which makes it
6 much more easier to park. The interior has been
7 specially designed with removable back seats. This
8 flexibility means it is a significantly more practical,
9 especially when you need a multi-purpose vehicle.
10 Last year it has won the annual industry award for safety innovation.

Unit 7
Outsourcing

www.longman-elt.com   www.economist.com

The great job migration

Keynotes

Globalisation is forcing businesses to make **cost savings** by reducing **operating costs**. One way to do this is by **outsourcing** – transferring **business processes** such as order processing or **call centre** management to outside suppliers and **service providers**. **Offshoring** is a new form of outsourcing where businesses relocate **back-office** operations in overseas **facilities** where **labour costs** are lower.

Outsourcing

Many companies are now setting up facilities in countries that can provide services at a far lower cost. What do you think the advantages and risks are of going offshore?

Listening 1 ⊙ Now listen to Lincoln Allenson, the director of an offshoring consultancy, and compare your answers. Listen again and make notes on the following.

1 the types of work that can easily transfer overseas
2 factors affecting the choice of location
3 the risks of outsourcing abroad

Speaking **1** Complete the table with the following countries.

India   Philippines   Ireland   USA

	1	2	3	4
Country	_____	_____	_____	_____
Average annual salary of programmer (US $)	70,000	29,000	10,000	6,500
Total workforce	140m	1.8m	439m	32m
No of university graduates (per year)	1.2m	30,000	700,000	380,000

2 How do you think these figures could influence companies considering outsourcing part of their operations?

Reading **Going offshore**

1 Read the text on the opposite page. What would be the advantages of offshoring for the following?

US companies   Indian companies   US workers   US consumers

2 Find the three examples in the text for each of the following.

1 phases of globalisation
   manufacturing jobs   _____   _____

2 factors driving offshoring
   _____   _____   _____

3 key qualities of host countries
   _____   _____   _____

The new global shift

The next round of globalization is under way. Who will the big winners be?

'The handwriting is on the wall,' writes an IT specialist at the Bank of America. Until recently the bank needed talent so badly it had to outbid rivals. But last fall, his entire 15-engineer team was told their jobs were redundant. Bank of America has already slashed 3,700 of its 25,000 technical and back-office jobs and more are to follow.

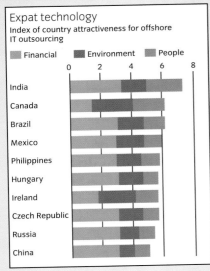

Expat technology
Index of country attractiveness for offshore IT outsourcing

■ Financial ■ Environment ■ People

0   2   4   6   8

India
Canada
Brazil
Mexico
Philippines
Hungary
Ireland
Czech Republic
Russia
China

Glossary

layoffs	redundancies
surplus	too much / many
backlash	strong negative reaction

AmE	vs	BrE
labor		labour
center		centre
fall		autumn
hiring		recruitment
transfered		transferred
college		university

Corporate downsizings are nothing new. These layoffs, though, aren't just happening because demand has dried up; one-third of those jobs are headed to India, where work that costs $100 an hour in the US gets done for $20. At Infosys Technologies Ltd. in Bangalore, India, 250 engineers are developing computer applications for Bank of America. About 1,600km north, at Wipro Spectramind Ltd., 2,500 young college-educated men and women are checking accident reports for an insurance company and providing help-desk support for a big internet service provider – all at a cost up to 60% lower than in the USA.

It's globalization's next phase – and one of the biggest trends reshaping the global economy. The first phase started two decades ago with the transfer of manufacturing jobs to economically developing countries. After that, simple service work, like processing credit card receipts, and digital labor, like writing software code, began fleeing high-cost countries.

Now, all kinds of knowledge work can be done almost anywhere. The driving forces are digitization, the internet, and high-speed data networks that circle the globe. By mining databases over the internet, offshore staff can check individuals' credit records, analyse corporate financial information, and search through oceans of economic statistics.

The impact of offshore hiring is hard to measure, since so far a tiny portion of US white-collar work has jumped overseas. Indeed, a case can be made that the US will see a net gain from this shift. In the 1990s, the USA had to import hundreds of thousands of immigrants to ease engineering shortages. Now, by sending routine service and engineering tasks to nations with a surplus of educated workers, the US labor force and capital can be redeployed to higher-value industries.

Globalization should also keep service prices in check, just as it did when manufacturing went offshore. Companies will be able to reduce overheads and improve efficiency. 'Our comparative advantage may shift to other fields,' says economist Robert Lipsey, 'and if productivity is high, then the US will maintain a high standard of living.' By encouraging economic development in nations such as India, meanwhile, US companies will have expanded foreign markets for their goods and services.

Outsourcing experts say the big job migration has only just begun. Frances Karamouzis, research director at Gartner Inc., expects 40% of the USA's top 1,000 companies to have an overseas pilot project under way within two years. The really big offshore push won't be until 2010 or so, she predicts. But if big layoffs result at home, corporations and the US government will face a backlash. Some states are already pushing for legislation to stop public jobs from being transfered overseas and now the unions are moving into the fight to keep jobs at home.

The truth is, the rise of the global knowledge industry is so recent that most economists haven't begun to understand the implications. For developing nations, the big beneficiaries will be those offering the speediest and cheapest telecom links, investor-friendly policies, and ample college graduates. In the West, it's far less clear who will be the big winners and losers. But we'll soon find out.

Speaking	**Can you think of any companies in your country going offshore?**

Offshoring

Complete the wordmap with the following words and phrases.

credit records   layoffs   overheads   high-speed data networks   backlash
labour costs   job creation   foreign markets   economic development
investor-friendly   efficiency   corporate financial information
internet   databases   demand   cheap telecoms

USA	India
_____	_____
_____	_____

Information sources
databases _____
_____
_____

Impacts

**Offshoring and the
global economy**

Technologies
_____
_____
_____

Economic factors
demand _____
_____
_____

Performance/objectives
improve _____
reduce _____
expand _____

Collocations

**Which expressions are used in the text on page 61 to describe the
following types of work?**

	verb	noun	
1	_develop_	_computer applications_	adapt software for new uses
2	_____	_____	deal with insurance payments
3	_____	_____	give customers assistance
4	_____	_____	record bank transactions
5	_____	_____	write in computer language
6	_____	_____	exploit data stored electronically
7	_____	_____	evaluate company results

Are these tasks simple service work or knowledge work?

Conditionals 1 and 2

Look at the following conditional sentences and complete the explanations below.

Type 1: *If big layoffs result at home, the US government will face a backlash.*

Type 2: *If US salaries were lower, companies wouldn't transfer work overseas.*

> unlikely to happen   may possibly happen   unreal   modal
> present tense   past tense   present tense   *would/could* + verb

- In type 1 conditionals the *if*-clause refers to a situation that _____.
  Type 1 conditionals are formed with *if* + _____* and the
  _____ or a _____ verb in the other half of the sentence.
- In type 2 conditionals the *if*-clause refers to a situation that is either
  _____ or _____. Type 2 conditionals are formed with *if* +
  _____ and _____ in the other half of the sentence.

*Although some modals are possible in an *if*-clause, do not use **will**.

 For more information, see page 160.

For more information, see page 160.

Practice

1 Decide which of these things may happen or are unlikely to happen. Write complete sentences using the appropriate verb forms.

1 if we / reduce / labour costs / be / more efficient

   If we reduce labour costs, we'll be more efficient.

   We'll be more efficient if we reduce labour costs.

2 if I / have / bigger salary / be / more motivated
3 if I / speak Chinese / need / translator
4 if I / have enough money / retire now
5 if I / meet / objectives / get / bonus
6 if I / see supervisor / I ask her a day off
7 if I / have / phone number / call / him
8 if I / work / this weekend / get / overtime

Speaking

2 Work in pairs. Find out what your partner would do in three of the following situations. Then answer your partner's questions.

1 your company asks you to work abroad for six months
2 you find out a colleague is selling copies of company software
3 you find out that you are being paid less than your colleagues
4 you realise that your credit card is missing
5 a colleague is criticising the quality of your work
6 your company asks you to go on a six-week intensive Chinese course

Working in India

1 Régis Sultan is a French computer engineer working in India. Listen to him talk about his job and choose the best option for questions 1–6.

1   Régis is working in a
   a   research centre.
   b   customer support service.
   c   production department.

2   It is difficult to recruit locally because there are
   a   not enough technically–qualified people.
   b   too many similar companies in the area.
   c   few candidates with good language skills.

3   How many hours a day does he work?
   a   six
   b   eight
   c   ten

4   When did he attend training courses?
   a   every evening
   b   at weekends
   c   every morning

5   Régis describes his colleagues as mostly
   a   male and female language graduates.
   b   men from non-technical professions.
   c   untrained female university graduates.

6   Where is he living?
   a   with an Indian family
   b   in a local hotel
   c   in a rented apartment

Régis Sultan

Speaking   **2** In the second part of the interview Régis talks about offshoring. What does he say about the following things?

1   why it is happening
2   the jobs offshoring creates
3   the future for Indian companies

Would you be interested in working in India? What terms and conditions would make you accept a job there?

Making and responding to suggestions

Choosing the right way to phrase suggestions depends on the context of the conversation. Being able to give an opinion about the best course of action or to advise someone about what you think they should do means using the appropriate language. You can do this by using the following phrases.

How/What about ... ?　　　　　　　*OK, let's do / try that.*
Couldn't you / we ... ?　　　　　　*Sounds good to me.*
Why don't you ... ?　　　　　　　*But what if ...?*
If I were you ...　　　　　　　　　*The only thing / problem is ...*
I suggest / think you should ...　　*It's a good idea, but ...*
It might be better to ...　　　　　*You're right.*

Listening 3 ⊙

1 Listen to six short dialogues in which people make suggestions. Match the dialogues with the topics a–f.

			phrases	responses
a	☐	being late for work	_____	_____
b	☐	work scheduling	_____	_____
c	1	a job interview	*Well, if I were you ...*	*But what if ...?*
d	☐	choosing a venue	_____	_____
e	☐	performance	_____	_____
f	☐	the agenda	_____	_____

⊙ **2** Listen again. Which phrases do the speakers use to make and respond to suggestions?

Speaking

Work in pairs. Think of a difficult situation that you have had to face recently. Explain the problem to your partner and ask them to make suggestions about what to do.

Culture at work

Decision-making

In some cultures senior managers make decisions and others carry out their instructions. In other cultures decisions are made by consensus after everyone contributes suggestions and opinions. What is common in your country? How might this difference cause misunderstanding in multicultural teams?

Dilemma & Decision

Dilemma: Going offshore

Brief

InterState, Inc. is a New York based company specialised in providing domestic insurance for private individuals and small corporations. InterState is currently considering outsourcing all or part of its 150-person call centre to an overseas location in order to reduce its operating costs. The call centre currently processes calls from both insurance agents and enquiries from members of the public within the USA. Several groups of managers have been asked to research different host countries in order to evaluate their potential to host a pilot project which should be operational within the next six months. If successful, the centre would take over full responsibility for all call centre operations within twelve months. The management teams will be meeting later in the day to present their recommendations. The following countries have been selected as potential hosts.

Fact file	China	India	Philippines	Canada
Population	1,275m	1,009m	76m	31m
% under 15	25%	34%	38%	20%
% in tertiary education	6%	7%	28%	58%
GP per head	$860	$450	$990	$22,370
Cost of living (USA = 100)	96	39	42	73
Competitiveness (World rank)	31	42	40	8
Operating costs (Japan = 100)	9	8	n/a	46

Task 1

Work in groups. Read the fact file and compare the advantages and disadvantages of each country as a call centre location.

Task 2

Prepare the recommendations that your group will make at the meeting.

Task 3

Present your findings to the group. Listen to the presentations made by the other groups. Discuss the recommendations together and reach a final decision about where to host the pilot project.

Write it up

Write a formal report to the management board. Compare your own country with your chosen offshore location and recommend what action InterState should take. (See Style guide, page 28.)

Useful phrases

Why don't we ... ?

I think we should ...

It might be better if we ...

I suggest we ...

Decision:

Dilip Patel is an economic analyst at the Institute for Labour Studies in London. Listen to him talk about the InterState situation and find out what he would recommend.

Unit 8
Finance

www.longman-elt.com   www.economist.com

The bottom line

FOR SALE
more information @
www.studio8.net
comedy that's funny

Keynotes

Huge losses experienced by investors and employees due to **mismanagement** and **irregularities** in **financial reporting** have led to a demand for stricter corporate governance. Independent **auditors** such as the **SEC** (Securities and Exchange Commission) in the US have been checking **balance sheets**, which show the overall performance of companies and **income statements** (AmE) or **profit and loss accounts** (BrE) which show the difference between total income and **outgoings** for a given period.

The Profit and Loss Account (P&L)

Study the incomplete P&L below. Complete the document with the following headings. Use a dictionary to help you.

Research and development costs   Cost of materials   Gross profit
Interest receivable   Turnover   Dividend

Consolidated Profit and Loss

for the year ended Dec 31 in $m

	Forecast	Actual
Money in ——— 1 _____ (sales revenue)	700	704
Other earnings		
Gains on fixed assets and operations	250	244
2 _____ on investments	175	162
Money out ——— **Costs of making goods**		
3 _____ and all manufacturing expenses	(100)	a _____
Salaries and personnel costs	(200)	b _____
Money in minus cost of making goods ——— 4 _____	825	c _____
Other money out ——— **Other costs and expenses**		
Indirect costs or overheads	(25)	(22)
5 _____	(50)	d _____
Loss on fixed assets	(25)	(25)
Loss on foreign operations	(100)	(88)
Marketing and distribution costs	(100)	e _____
Gross profit minus other money out ——— **Trading/Operating Profit**	525	f _____
Profit for shareholders (6 _____)	95	g _____
Money left when shareholders have been paid ——— **Retained profit**	430	h _____

Listening

1 Now listen to a presentation of the actual results and complete the missing figures for gaps a–h.

2 Listen again and answer the following questions.

1 Why was gross profit higher than expected?
2 Where did the company decide to have parts made?
3 Which budgets went over the forecast limits?
4 What is expected to happen to the marketing budget in future?
5 How much will shareholders receive per share?
6 What prediction does the speaker make about retained profit?

Speaking **If you were a potential shareholder would you feel confident in investing in this company? Why? / Why not?**

Listening 2

Creative accounting

1 Companies sometimes make the figures in financial documents more attractive than they really are. They can do this by:

a inventing revenues from companies that don't exist
b not including debts of subsidiaries and acquisitions
c hiding debts on the books of subsidiaries
d overstating current profits by including possible future earnings

Listen to two investors talk about what happened to them when they invested in two media companies. Which of the above methods were used to drive up share prices in each case?

2 Listen again and complete the graphs.

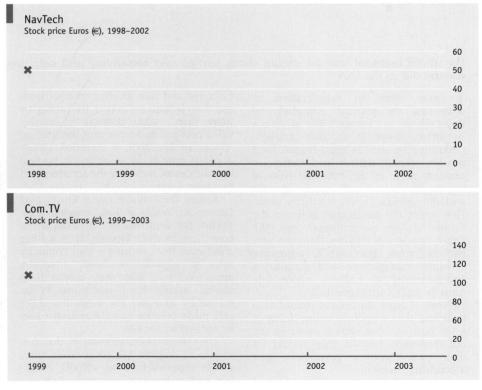

NavTech
Stock price Euros (€), 1998–2002

Com.TV
Stock price Euros (€), 1999–2003

Speaking **Can you think of any other famous financial scandals?**

Corporate governance

Read the text about corporate governance. What accounting irregularities are mentioned? Who was responsible?

The Economist

Glossary

overwhelming   too large to deal with

absolves   removes responsibility

Corporate governance

Europe's Enron

The Ahold financial scandal should shock Europe into accounting and corporate governance reform, just as the Enron scandal did in the USA.

It may seem an exaggeration to describe the scandal overwhelming Royal Ahold as "Europe's Enron" – but in many ways it is true enough. Certainly, the world's third-biggest food retailer, after Wal-Mart and Carrefour, presents none of the financial risks of Enron, which was both deeply in debt and the world's largest electricity giant. That apart, the similarities between the former Texan powerhouse and the Dutch retailer are striking, from the very bad corporate governance, aggressive earnings management and accounting "irregularities" to auditors whose role must be called into question.

Now, at least, Europeans should stop believing that corporate wrong-doing is a US problem that cannot occur in the old continent. Instead, they should fix their own corporate governance and accounting problems.

On 24 February 2003 Ahold announced the resignation of its chief executive and finance director after finding that it had overstated its profits by more than 463m ($500m). Its market value plunged by 63 per cent that day, to 3.3bn. In late 2001, it exceeded 30bn. Ahold is now under investigation by various authorities, including the Securities and Exchange Commission (SEC) in the USA.

Rather like Kenneth Lay at Enron, and Dennis Kozlowski at Tyco, another scandal-hit US firm, Ahold's now-departing boss, Cees van der Hoeven, won a huge reputation from turning a dull company into a growth machine. Investors applauded long after they should have started asking hard questions. When eventually they did ask them, his anger and pride became quickly apparent and he refused to answer.

The 463m overstatement is due primarily to Ahold's US Foodservice unit, which supplies food to schools, hospitals and restaurants, although there are also issues over its Disco subsidiary in Argentina and several other units. This has led some observers to say that this is less a European problem than yet another US accounting failure. Such a claim absolves Ahold's bosses of responsibility for their acquisitions and dishonesty and ignores the persistent, firm-wide tendency to test the limits of acceptable accounting.

Most firms that buy in bulk – including such admired retailers as Wal-Mart and Tesco – get discounts from suppliers if they meet sales targets. The issue is how those rebates are accounted for. The accepted practice is to wait until the targets are met. Failing firms, such as now-bankrupt Kmart, food distributor Fleming, and now Ahold appear to have booked these rebate payments before they were earned.

What of Ahold's auditor? Although the problems were uncovered, it should have done so much earlier, says Lynn Turner, a former chief accountant at the SEC ■

2 **Read the text again and answer the following questions.**

1 What are the similarities between Enron and Ahold?
2 What should European companies do?
3 Why did the shareholders admire Cees van der Hoeven?
4 Which of Ahold's acquisitions is mentioned in the text?
5 What did Europeans believe about corporate wrong-doing in the past?
6 How did Foodservice overstate its sales?

Speaking Do you think CEOs who falsify accounts are criminals and should go to jail or is it an acceptable risk to falsify accounts if it helps to safeguard the company's future and jobs?

Vocabulary **Choose the best word to fill each gap in the sentences below.**

1 Sales are a good way for _____ to get rid of surplus stock.
   a retailers   b sellers   c dealers   d wholesalers

2 The company was in fact seriously _____ even though they claimed to be making a profit.
   a at a loss   b in debt   c in the black   d broken

3 Some companies _____ their earnings to drive up share prices.
   a overdo   b overflow   c overstate   d oversee

4 The Financial Services Authority was set up in the UK to deal with _____ such as fraud and insider trading.
   a issues   b ideas   c reasons   d purposes

5 When the CEO should have been cost cutting, he was spending huge sums on _____ that turned out to be unprofitable.
   a increases   b investors   c growth   d acquisitions

6 When you buy in bulk you can obtain _____ or rebates.
   a discounts   b sales   c decreases   d interest

7 Shareholders lost money when the company declared itself _____.
   a redundant   b sold out   c broken down d bankrupt

8 When they heard about our financial difficulties our _____ asked to be paid in advance.
   a service   b deliveries   c suppliers   d orders

9 They didn't lie – they simply tried to _____ the truth.
   a conceal   b prevent   c reduce   d warn

Adjectives and adverbs

Look at the following uses of adjectives.

– before nouns

There was a **dramatic** fall in profits last year.

– after stative verbs such as be, become, seem, appear, look, etc.

The similarities between Ahold and Enron are **striking**.

Look at the following uses of adverbs.

– after verbs

Shares fell **sharply** on the news.

– before an adjective or adverb

... his anger and pride became **quickly** apparent ...

For more information, see page 160.

Practice

1 Use the following expressions to describe the performance of the Enron share price 1991–2001.

fluctuated mildly   a sharp increase   reached a peak
rose steadily   dropped slightly   a dramatic and sudden fall

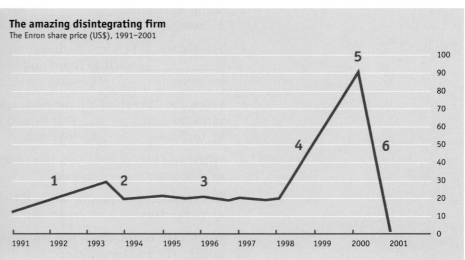

The amazing disintegrating firm
The Enron share price (US$), 1991–2001

2 Journalists use dramatic verbs that describe the direction, speed and degree of change. What information do these verbs give?

	direction	speed	large/small degree
plunge	↓	very fast	very large
dip	↓	fast	small
soar			
plummet			
slide			
skyrocket			
jump			
nosedive			
decline			

Referring to visuals

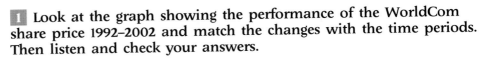

Visual aids such as graphs, bar charts, pie charts and flow charts are an important and effective way of structuring and communicating presentations that include a lot of statistics. The following phrases are useful for drawing the listeners' attention to particular details.

As you can see, ...	*... led to the ... you see here ...*
You'll notice that, ...	*... is obvious on this part of the graph here.*
This part of the graph clearly shows ...	*This slide shows the ...*

Listening 3 ⊙

WorldCom
Share price (US$), 1992–2002

1 Look at the graph showing the performance of the WorldCom share price 1992–2002 and match the changes with the time periods. Then listen and check your answers.

1	reached a record high	a	1992–95
2	nosedived to an all-time low	b	1995–98
3	continued to skyrocket	c	1998–99
4	started a spectacular ascension	d	1999
5	there was a downturn	e	1999–02

2 Work in pairs. Student A turn to page 139. Student B look at the bar chart showing the American sales of the Italian food giant Parmalat, which went bankrupt in 2003 with debts of €14bn. Describe the chart to your partner. Then listen to your partner and complete the European sales 1996–2003.

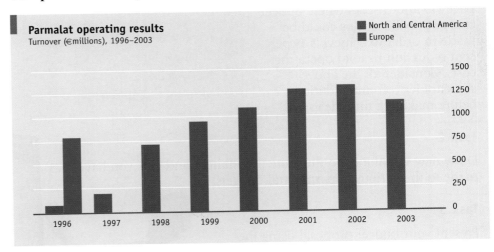

Parmalat operating results
Turnover (€millions), 1996–2003

■ North and Central America
■ Europe

Culture at work

Formal and informal presentations

Some cultures expect presentations to be formal and technical. Others find this dull and ineffective and prefer a more entertaining style of presentation. What are they like in your country? How might these attitudes affect the dress, style and use of visual aids in presentations in different countries?

Dilemma &Decision

Dilemma: Counting the costs

Brief

MultiBrands is a globally successful consumer products company, which has built up a reputation based on 'Honesty, Quality and Innovation'. Since it started operating ten years ago, it has launched at least two new, high-quality products in different markets every year. However, managers are currently reviewing company policy because of a recent dramatic fall in profits and share price performance. Shareholders believe that this is due to over-diversification, rising costs and failing consumer confidence as a result of complaints that product quality is declining. Shareholder recommendations are:

- freeze current policy of developing new products
- concentrate on consolidating current successful brands
- improve quality or reduce prices
- freeze recruitment but avoid layoffs
- reduce current budget by 15 per cent

Task 1

In groups, study the information on page 140 and discuss where budget cuts and reallocations could be made in order to achieve a 15 per cent reduction in total operating costs. Consider all the above shareholder recommendations before making a final decision.

> **Useful phrases**
>
> As you can see, ...
> You'll notice that ...
> ... clearly shows ...
> ... led to the ... you see here

Task 2

Draw new visual aids to illustrate the changes and cuts you have made to the various departmental budgets.

Task 3

Present your budget proposal using the new visual aids.

Write it up

Summarise your proposal in a short report. Include graphs and charts to help illustrate and support your ideas. (See Style guide, page 26.)

Decision:

- Listen to William Grange, from International Consultants, saying where he would have made the necessary budget adjustments and cuts.

Unit 9 Recruitment

www.longman-elt.com www.economist.com

Hiring for the future

Keynotes

Human resources departments are responsible for recruiting new **personnel**. **Candidates** are initially asked to provide a **curriculum vitae** (CV) or **resumé** (AmE) which gives information about their **qualifications**, **experience** and **skills**. The recruiter then **screens** the **applications** and selects candidates for interview. Successful applicants are **hired** and put on the **payroll**.

The application process

When did you last apply for a job? What steps were involved in your application? Did you attend an interview? What sort of questions were you asked?

Kevin Quinlan, a Human Resources consultant, talks about three different types of job interview. Listen and complete the table.

Type of interview	1a_____	2a_____	3a_____
Type of questions	b_____	b_____	anecdotal
Information gained	• qualifications c_____ • knowledge d_____	• ability to analyse • formulate questions c_____	b_____ • ability to handle relationships

Imagine you were given responsibility for hiring several thousand employees for a new hotel in a short period of time. How would you organise the recruitment process?

Speed hiring

1 Read the jumbled text on the opposite page and arrange the extracts in the correct order.

2 Match the subheadings with paragraphs A–E.

1 Speed interviewing   _____
2 Click to file   _____
3 Checking in and checking out _____
4 Empower your managers   _____
5 Making yourself redundant   _____

3 What do the following numbers refer to in the text?

1 24 weeks   *the time available for recruiting new staff*
2 740   _____
3 20 per cent   _____
4 30 minutes   _____
5 8 per cent   _____
6 $1.9 million _____

A Full House

Recruiting the entire staff for the Bellagio hotel in Las Vegas in record time and at minimum cost may sound like mission impossible. But Arte Nathan came up trumps.

Talk about long odds. Arte Nathan was Vice President of Human Resources for the launch of the Bellagio in Las Vegas. Everything about Bellagio was larger than life. So too was the challenge that confronted Nathan: hire 9,600 workers in 24 weeks. Nathan and his HR team would have to screen 84,000 applicants in 12 weeks, interview 27,000 finalists in 10 weeks, and process 9,600 hires in 11 days. In the end, they nailed the deadline and here's how they did it.

A This started out as an experiment. But in the end, the guinea pig survived. We saved Bellagio $1.9 million. Most HR people are afraid to let go of their hire-and-fire authority. But if you really want to sit at the big table, you've got to start thinking strategically and globally. And the only way to do that is to eliminate HR transactions from your life. You have to be willing to say, 'I am in the wrong place in this process.' You have to take yourself out of the system.

B If a manager wanted to hire you, he would click on CONDUCT BACKGROUND CHECK. Law-enforcement officials would then receive your application online and check your employment and education history. We rejected about eight per cent of our candidates at this stage for various reasons, such as lying on their applications. If you passed this and a drug test, the manager would then make the final decision. When you appoint somebody, you create three files: a personnel file, an equal employment opportunity commission file and a medical file. Why not have an electronic personnel file? In the process, we could eliminate the files that managers usually keep at their desks. So we developed one and transmitted everything from the application database to the new-hire database. Using the same technology for all of our personnel and payroll forms meant that we no longer had to collect, input, and file thousands of paper forms.

C The only way to hire so many so fast was to move everything online. That meant we had to build an online job application and HR system. I told our managers that this technology would give them hire-and-fire responsibility, which they say they want, and complete authority, which they rarely get. And it would make them 100 per cent accountable for their decisions. Going online would take human resources out of the process.

D Next came the interviews. Every day, 180 hiring managers, who we had specially trained, conducted 740 interviews of 30 minutes each. Applicants were asked a set of behavioral questions that we had developed, like 'Tell me about a time when you were at the front desk, and a guest was late. What did you do when you couldn't find the reservation?' Using a PC embedded in their desktops the managers evaluated the answers on a rating sheet and the scores were fed into the database.

E In 14 months we had designed, built, and implemented the system. This is how it worked: to apply for a position, you set up an appointment. When you arrived, an HR staff person wearing a microphone confirmed your identity and notified staff, who greeted you by name and assigned you to a computer terminal. Once you completed the application, the computer would ask you to proceed to a checkout desk where a staff member would review it. In fact what our people were really doing was assessing your communication skills and your overall demeanor. At that point, we weeded out about 20 per cent of the applicants.

Glossary

long odds little chance

nail the deadline meet a deadline

demeanor behaviour and looks

weed out to eliminate

guinea pig person used for a test

What do you think of the recruitment methods used at the Bellagio? Would you like to be recruited in this way?

Vocabulary 1

The two lists below show the Bellagio recruitment process from the viewpoint of the applicants and the HR team. Complete the lists with one of the following words.

> deadline train appointment computer application
> identity checkout conduct interview backgrounds
> test screen files system

Applicants

1 set up an _____
2 have staff confirm _____
3 enter data on a _____ terminal
4 complete the _____
5 proceed to _____
6 attend an _____
7 take a drug _____

The HR team

1 fix a _____ to complete each phase
2 design a computer _____
3 _____ all applications
4 _____ hiring managers
5 _____ interviews with candidates
6 check candidates' _____
7 create personnel _____

Vocabulary 2

Word-building

Read these definitions of words from the text. Write the word in the appropriate column and complete the other two columns.

	verb	noun	person
1 make a formal request	*apply*	*application*	*applicant*
2 test of someone's skills	_____	_____	_____
3 ask a candidate questions	_____	_____	_____
4 make a plan for something that will be built	_____	_____	_____
5 evaluate	_____	_____	_____
6 process by which people exchange information	_____	_____	_____
7 choose someone for a position	_____	_____	_____

Relative pronouns

We use the relative pronouns **which, that, who, whom, whose** to give additional information about somebody or something already mentioned. There are two different types.

1 **Defining clauses** give information which defines or differentiates the person or thing that they refer to.

*... an HR staff person wearing a microphone confirmed your identity and notified staff, **who** greeted you by name ...*

*Applicants were asked a set of questions (**that**) we had developed ...*

In the second sentence we can delete the pronoun *that* as it refers to the object and not the subject of the verb developed.

2 **Non-defining clauses** just give extra information and do not define what they refer to. This extra information appears between commas.

*... this technology would give them hire-and-fire responsibility, **which** they say they want, and complete authority, **which** they rarely get.*

 For more information, see page 160.

Practice

1 Look at the sentences below. Are the clauses defining or non-defining? Which pronouns can be deleted?

1 A major problem that we face is finding replacements for key personnel.

2 The latest survey, which was published last week, shows that there is a shortage of skilled workers.

3 We selected five of the twenty candidates who initially applied.

4 The applications that we have received so far are mostly from candidates with little or no experience.

5 We've rejected all applicants whose CVs had basic spelling mistakes.

6 Lyn Jackson, whose contribution to this project has been exceptional, will be leaving us in June.

2 Complete the extract from a company newsletter with appropriate relative pronouns. In some cases more than one answer is possible. Where could the relative pronouns be omitted?

Sammy Moreno

Sammy Moreno has been appointed Human Resources Director for Europe and takes over from Rosa Wasserman [1] __who__ retires at the end of April. Sammy, [2] _____ career has included key strategic assignments in both Latin America and Asia, doesn't underestimate the challenges [3] _____ lie ahead. 'This is a difficult time for organisations like ours [4] _____ are working to consolidate positions on the European market.' he says. 'The new regulations and legislation [5] _____ have been introduced recently, will complicate the task of co-ordinating the policies

[6] _____ the group can apply in individual countries on the continent.' Sammy, [7] _____ responsibilities will include providing policies, assistance and guidelines to regional HR directors is nonetheless optimistic: 'I'm hoping that with the new guidelines [8] _____ we will shortly be introducing, HR will be better positioned to do the job [9] _____ it's supposed to do – looking after the interests of the group as a whole and also of all our staff [10] _____ dedication and professionalism have put us in the leading position [11] _____ we are in today.'

The Curriculum Vitae (CV)

Read the following CV of Monika Vaz, who is applying for a position as a marketing manager. Listen to the questions that she is asked during an interview and fill in the missing information.

Monika Vaz

Hermanstrasse 16
Köln, 50858 Germany
Tel : 0049 221 5036887
E-mail: mvaz@cybermail.com

Objective: Seeking a position of responsibility in the field of Direct/Internet Marketing

Employment History

2004 to date: [1]_____
Phoenix Media , Hamburg, Germany
Planned and developed direct mail campaigns for major clients in the retail sector. Advised on internet marketing strategies. Conducted in-depth
[2]_____. Organised company participation at various media and direct mail events and [3]_____ of Phoenix products and services.

2003 – 2004: Assistant Sales Manager.
MSV – Business Services.
Amsterdam, Netherlands
Responsible for finding new clients, managing key accounts and
[4]_____.

Qualifications

2000 – 2003: Graduated from the University of Vienna with an Honours Degree in Sales Management.
Main course components: sales and marketing, accounting, European business law, media studies, economics, and information technology. Options:
[5]_____ and _____.
Awarded high school leaving certificate from the Vienna Schule, majoring in economics.

Other skills

Computers: Experience in programming in [6]_____, Flash and Dreamweaver. MS Office. SAP.
Languages: Mother tongue German, fluent French and English,
[7]_____ in Italian.

Personal Interests

Sports: [8]_____ and snowboarding. **Hobbies:** music (jazz piano) and theatre (member of an amateur theatre group).

References

- **Professor Jürgen Drexler**, University of Vienna.
- **Norman Achilles**, President of the European Marketing Foundation.

Writing Write a similar short CV for yourself.

Proof reading Making basic errors on your CV or application letter can ruin your chances of getting a job. Find and correct the following mistakes.

1 One of my qualities is that I am very atentive to small details.
2 I hope you will be able to arrange to interview me shorty.
3 For me there are no bariers to quality.
4 I hope that you will find the time to overlook my CV.
5 For three years I was ruining the entire department.
6 I think I have excellent keybored skills.

Smalltalk

Business meetings, telephone calls and interviews often involve smalltalk – chatting informally about unrelated topics of common interest. Work in pairs. Try to explain one of the following to your partner. Was it hard keeping the conversation going? Why?

- something that happened to you
- a newspaper story you read recently

1 Look at the list of short utterances used to show we are listening. What do they tell the speaker?

Right   OK   No!   Sure   Wow!   Really?   You're kidding!

2 Sometimes we need to give the speaker further encouragement by asking questions. Match the following questions to the functions.

a   encourage the speaker to continue
b   check our understanding
c   express our feelings

1   So then what did you do?
2   What exactly do you mean by that?
3   That wasn't very helpful, was it?
4   Then what happened?
5   Sorry, what did you say?
6   How could you do a thing like that?

3 It's also important to close a conversation at the right moment and in the right way. Here are examples of the way people do this.

1   I'm terribly sorry but I really have to go now.
2   Why don't I give you a call and we can arrange to meet?
3   Look at the time! I didn't realise it was so late. I'd better be off.
4   Nice talking to you. See you sometime soon.
5   I don't want to keep you any longer.
6   Well, I guess I'd better be going. Take care.

Speaking

Work in pairs. Start a conversation and continue it for at least one minute. Use the topics below or your own. Did you learn anything about the other person? How did your conversation end?

films   books   music   television   travel   famous people

Culture at work   ## Attitudes to personal space

In some cultures people require little personal space. They stand close together, touch each other often and are happy to discuss personal matters. This can make people from other cultures feel very uncomfortable. How much personal space do people in your country need? How might this difference cause misunderstanding in multicultural teams?

Dilemma & Decision

Dilemma: The Bellagio interview

Brief

You are members of the HR team that is responsible for the recruitment drive at the Bellagio. You have been asked to design the list of questions for the behavioural interview that will be used by all the hiring managers. This interview will last a maximum of 30 minutes and will contain six questions designed to evaluate the behaviour of the candidates. After each question the hiring manager will enter an evaluation of the quality of the candidate's response directly into a computer. The HR team have agreed that the questions should focus on as many of the following areas as possible:

Conflict — will he/she get on with other people?
Authority — will he/she respect authority?
Ambition — is he/she interested in career development?
Networking — is he/she able to develop and maintain contacts?
Sociability — will he/she mix easily with other people?
Appearance — is this important to the candidate?
Stress — can he/she operate under stress?
Resourcefulness — can he/she handle unexpected situations?

Task 1

Work in groups. Prepare the list of questions that you will give to the HR managers. Decide the order in which the questions will be asked and prepare an evaluation grid for the managers to enter their marks out of five. (5 = excellent.)

Task 2

Work in pairs. Test your questions by role-playing a test interview.

Write it up

How did the interview go? Are there any changes that you need to make to your questions? Now prepare an email to send to the hiring managers with your questions and expected responses.

Decision:

⊙ Listen to what Joyce Carolan, an HR consultant, thinks about how the interview should be designed.

Review 3

Language check

Conditionals 1 and 2

Complete the sentences with the correct form of the verbs in brackets.

1 If prices (continue) _____ to fall this way, we (not / make) _____ a profit this year.

2 If they (go) _____ into China, they (certainly / find) _____ cheaper labour, but they think it's too big a risk.

3 I (not / buy) _____ shares in a company if its balance sheet (not / be) _____ healthy.

4 If the company (not / show) _____ a profit this year, the shareholders (ask) _____ for a vote of confidence at the next annual meeting.

5 I (apply) _____ for the job if I (have) _____ the qualifications, but I don't.

6 If I (be) _____ him, I (step) _____ down before the scandal hits the newspapers.

Adjectives and adverbs

Complete the sentences with the correct form of the words in brackets.

1 The similarities between the WorldCom and Parmalat financial disasters are really quite (striking) _____ .

2 He said shares are up $5 from last week and that is a pretty (dramatic) _____ rise.

3 Changes in financial trends are so (fast) _____ nowadays that I can't keep up with them.

4 I lost a lot of money when share prices fell (sharp) _____ last year.

5 After years of stagnation their share price is finally beginning to increase but the pace is so (slow) _____ it'll take time to make any real money.

6 You should buy now that prices are down but act fast as things are moving very (quick)_____.

7 The FSA launched an enquiry after their share price started to rise (surprise)_____ quickly.

8 The performance of their overseas subsidiaries has been (disappointing) _____ this year.

9 Turnover dipped (slight) _____ due to the weak dollar.

10 Profits were down due to a (steady) _____ rise in our operating costs.

Relative pronouns

Complete the sentences with a relative pronoun where necessary.

1 We really liked the candidate _____ application came late.

2 He is presently working at a company _____ you used to work for.

3 The candidates _____ we saw earlier didn't have enough experience in our field.

4 Apparently you're the person _____ told him we were looking for someone.

5 As there are two positions vacant I'm not sure _____ would suit you best.

6 Do you know anyone else _____ might be interested in the other post?

Consolidation

Underline the correct forms of the words in *italics*.

Five years ago the general public still believed companies were responsible social citizens. Now CEOs have to prove that it is not they [1]*that / who* have personally ruined and bankrupted companies. If they [2]*will respect / respect* the new regulatory laws they [3]*will / would* no longer be free to do what they want but they [4]*will / would* be held accountable for their actions.

In the USA, it is the Securities and Exchange Commission (SEC) [5]*which / who* regulates company auditing. Since Enron they have [6]*dramatic / dramatically* [7]*risen / increased* the number of companies [8]*which / whose* audits they say need correcting. In the UK, the Financial Services Authority (FSA) says it [9]*would / will* start searching actively for irregular accounting practices if the current [10]*rise / grow up* in the number of financial scandals [11]*continues / continued*.

However, there are no easy solutions; if the new rules [12]*were / are* applied [13]*would they / will they* improve corporate governance? Ultimately, the best way to prevent share prices [14]*plummeting / skyrocketing* is to have directors [15]*who / which* are willing to stake their reputations on their job. And no rules can guarantee that.

Vocabulary check

Complete the text with the correct option A–C.

Manufacturers have used foreign [1]_____ for years. But now, companies are also looking abroad for service [2]_____ in countries where labour costs are low. Growing pressure to produce healthy [3]_____ sheets and increased profits every year, means companies are seeking to [4]_____ people in cheaper markets.

India, with a large pool of workers who have the required [5]_____, low wages and English language is particularly popular with US companies wishing to offshore some of their key business [6]_____.

There are fears that corporate [7]_____ will lead to a protectionist mood in economically developed countries. However, economists claim that the job [8]_____ will benefit everyone as greater efficiency means lower prices. But [9]_____ for service jobs in the UK and US are finding it harder to secure work these days and therefore have trouble seeing the immediate advantages of [10]_____ abroad.

1	A makers	B suppliers	C operators
2	A providers	B facilitators	C processors
3	A financial	B profit	C balance
4	A hire	B market	C resource
5	A qualifications	B papers	C certificates
6	A tasks	B systems	C processes
7	A downsizing	B reductions	C shrinkings
8	A sourcing	B demand	C migration
9	A applicants	B candidates	C interviewees
10	A outputting	B outplacing	C outsourcing

Career skills

Making suggestions

Complete the dialogue with the following phrases.

how about   why don't you   if I were you
you might be better off

A I'm sick of hotel work. I wish I could have a career change.

B [1]_____ look at the job offers in the papers?

A But I'd probably need to retrain first. I've never worked in any other field.

B [2]_____ I would think about areas related to your present qualifications.

A Like what?

B [3]_____ another aspect of tourism, like tour operator or tour guide for example.

A That's a good idea, I would really like to keep using my foreign language skills.

B Well, in that case, [4]_____ looking at the possibility of translating or interpreting too.

Referring to visuals

Complete the description of the graph with the following words and phrases.

a soar
b steady climb
c peak
d slide
e gradual increase
f nosedive

Share price 1999-2003

$30 / 20 / 10
99 00 01 02 03 04 05

As you can see, the share price stood at $10 per share in 1999. Shareholders were happy to see a [1]_____ to $20 from 1999 to 2001. However, here we notice that the threat of closure of one of our important foreign subsidiaries caused a [2]_____ and shares were back down to $6 by the end of 2002 where they stayed until the takeover of our biggest competitor which caused the share price to [3]_____ before reaching a [4]_____ in 2003. Unfortunately it proved to be very difficult and expensive to make the new operation profitable and this inevitably led to a [5]_____ in share prices. Since then we have been experiencing steady growth and similarly the share price is starting a [6]_____, a trend we hope will continue.

Smalltalk

Underline the incorrect extra word in each sentence in the dialogue.

A How was your trip about?

B Fantastic lots. In fact, I'm be thinking of asking for a transfer. I'd love to work there for a while ago.

A Really true?

B Yeah, really, our team there is so much dynamic and the social life is great.

A Sounds ideal, when would you like to leave it?

B Well, I have to finish at my project here first, so it depends on how much time that takes.

A Yeah, well, I don't want to keep you any more longer, so let me know how it goes.

Unit 10
Counterfeiting

www.longman-elt.com   www.economist.com

The globalisation of deceit

Keynotes

Counterfeiters ignore **patents**, which **protect intellectual property**, **copyright** and **trademarks**, by producing cheap copies or **fakes** of branded goods. These **infringements** are openly practised daily, affecting many businesses. **Digitisation** and the internet have made it easier than ever to mass reproduce and distribute quality counterfeit products. The music industry in particular claims to be losing millions because of **file sharing systems** which allow the **downloading** of music free of charge.

The universal crime?

Below is a list of copyright infringements. In pairs, rank them according to which ones you consider to be the most dishonest.

- buying a fake Rolex watch
- photocopying pages from a published book
- lending a book you enjoyed to a friend to read
- downloading music from an internet file-sharing system
- making a digital copy of a CD or DVD
- showing a video to a group of people for money

1 Listen to two people talk about counterfeiting. What examples of copyright infringement do they mention?

2 Listen again and answer the questions.

According to the first speaker:

1 How does counterfeiting benefit consumers?

2 Why would she buy copies of brands?

According to the second speaker:

1 Which industries are affected by the problem in the European Union?

2 What are the most serious consequences of counterfeiting?

3 How are high prices of branded goods justified?

3 Which of the speakers are you most likely to agree with? Why?

Copyright infringement

1 Quickly scan the text on the opposite page and underline examples of counterfeiting.

2 Complete the text with the following sentences.

a However, brand owners often willingly hand over production masters to counterfeiters without realising it.

b As long as there is a market for a product the copycats will imitate it.

c Peter Lowe, head of the CIB, reckons that some $25bn worth of counterfeit goods are traded each year over the internet.

d In recent years the counterfeiters have gone from strength to strength.

e Some of these, borrowed from security devices developed for use on dollar bills, are clearly visible and are intended to help consumers distinguish fakes from genuine goods.

f Procter & Gamble reckons it spends $3m a year fighting the copycats.

Glossary

churn out mass produce cheaply

vulnerable easy to attack

perpetrator criminal

sweatshops small factories with bad conditions

shoddy poor quality

flattery praise

Copyright infringement

Imitating property is theft

Counterfeiting is on the increase. Companies ignore it at their peril

To most people, counterfeiting means forged currency. But counterfeiters are copying an ever-widening range of products. For some time they have been churning out imitation designer fashion, software and CDs. Now they are copying medicines, mobile phones, food and drink, car parts and even tobacco. [1]

[2] New technology has broadened the range of goods that are vulnerable to copying. It has dramatically improved their quality, as well as lowering their cost of production. Where once counterfeits were cheap and shoddy imitations of the real thing, today their packaging and contents (especially for digital products such as software, music CDs and DVDs) often mean they are almost indistinguishable from the genuine article.

A counterfeit, by definition, is something that is copied or imitated without the perpetrator having the right to do it and with the purpose of deceiving or defrauding. Such rights are legally covered by patents (for inventions), copyright (for artistic works and software), trademarks (for words, pictures, symbols and industrial designs) and other forms of intellectual-property protection.

Counterfeiting is as diverse as any legal business, ranging from back-street sweatshops to full-scale factories. Counterfeiters often get their goods by bribing employees in a company with a valuable brand to hand over manufacturing moulds or master disks for them to copy. [3] One of the most frustrating problems for brand owners is when their licensed suppliers and manufacturers "over-run" production lines without permission and then sell the extra goods on the side.

Distribution networks can be as simple as a stall in the street, or a shop on the other side of the world. The internet has been a great help to counterfeiters, giving them detailed information about which goods to copy and allowing them to link consumers and suppliers with ease. [4]

Counterfeiting is not a victimless crime. For a start, legitimate businesses lose sales because of competition from counterfeiters. If their brand loses value (because it is seen as less exclusive or is confused with shoddy imitations), there is a long-term threat to profitability. In addition, firms have to bear the cost of anti-counterfeiting measures. [5] One strategy that companies increasingly use is to load their vulnerable products with anti-counterfeiting features. [6] Companies also use these features, primarily to help them track their products through the supply chain and to distinguish genuine articles from fakes, especially should they need to take the copycats to court. But no amount of effort will ever completely stop the copycats. For as long as there is consumer demand, companies will find that imitation is the severest form of flattery ∎

3 **Read the text again and answer the following questions.**

1 What role has technology played in the expansion of counterfeiting?
2 How do counterfeiters often obtain their production masters?
3 What are the distribution networks for counterfeit products?
4 What effects does counterfeiting have on legal businesses?

Vocabulary 1 **Counterfeiting**

Choose the best word to complete each sentence.

1 Expensive _____ fashion items are commonly copied products.
   a excluded   b invented   c designer   d prototype

2 Copies are so well made that they are almost _____ from the original.
   a identical   b the same   c incomparable   d indistinguishable

3 Many consumers prefer to pay more for a _____ brand.
   a genuine   b right   c normal   d reality

4 _____ manufacturers receive permission to produce branded goods.
   a Partner   b Associated   c Agreed   d Licensed

5 The overseas printer produced extra books and sold them _____.
   a on the side   b besides   c inside   d over the side

6 The music industry is very concerned about _____ infringement.
   a patent   b copyright   c trademark   d intellectual

7 Increased counterfeiting affects the brand owners' future _____.
   a balancing   b potential   c profitability   d finance

8 CDs and Videos are particularly _____ to piracy.
   a easy   b suspect   c vulnerable   d valuable

9 One legal action against counterfeiters is to take them to _____.
   a justice   b court   c account   d copyright

Vocabulary 2 **Prefixes**

Form the opposites of these adjectives and adverbs by adding *in-*, *un-* or *il-*. Use a dictionary to help you.

1 distinguishable   *indistinguishable*
2 vulnerable   _____
3 legitimate   _____
4 profitable   _____
5 legally   _____
6 willingly   _____
7 visible   _____

Conditionals 1–3

1 **Study these examples of conditional sentences and answer the questions below.**

a   If there is high consumer demand for a brand it **will be** vulnerable to counterfeiting. (Type 1)

b   If so much of a product's worth **wasn't** tied up in brand and intellectual property it **wouldn't be** so easy to sell poor quality substitutes. (Type 2)

c   If we **hadn't produced** overseas, we **wouldn't have had** the pirate copies flooding the market. (Type 3)

1   Does each example refer to past, present or future time?

2   In c did the company produce overseas?

3   In c did pirate copies flood the market?

4   Which examples refer to a situation that is unreal or unlikely to happen?

5   Which example refers to a situation that is likely to happen?

2 **Match the two halves to form the correct conditional forms.**

Type 1:   if + a present tense,   a   would / could + verb

Type 2:   if + a past tense,   b   would / could have + past participle

Type 3:   if + had + past participle, c   present tense or modal verb

 For more information, see page 160.

For more information, see page 160.

Practice

Complete the sentences with the correct forms of the verbs.

1   If I (have) _'d had_____ enough money, I (buy) _'d have bought_ a real Rolex but I just didn't, so I bought a fake.

2   If local counterfeiters only (pay) _____ a fine of $1,000 when they are caught they (keep on) _____ producing counterfeit goods.

3   There (not / be) _____ so many imitation drugs on the market if the prices of the genuine products (not / be) _____ so high.

4   If we (not / drop) _____ our prices in the region I think we (be) _____ vulnerable to counterfeiting by local companies.

5   We (not / manufacture) _____ locally if we (not / trust) _____ them to produce only the agreed quantities. It's been fine so far.

6   If I (know) _____ it was a fake, I (not / buy) _____ it.

7   We're considering introducing some sophisticated anti-counterfeiting features but it (cost) _____ a lot of money if we (use) _____ them.

8   I (not / work) _____ for a counterfeiter if I (can / get) _____ another job elsewhere, but I can't.

Speaking

Work in pairs. Find out what your partner would have done in the following situations.

–   if they hadn't come to school / work today

–   if they had met their favourite celebrity in a café this morning

–   if they had been offered pirate copies of their favourite music at $5 a CD

The music industry

1 Listen to Gilles Philips, a journalist, talk about the effects of file-swapping technology on the music industry. What does he think are the reasons for the industry's recent poor performance?

2 Listen again and choose the best option for questions 1–6.

1 Which of the following is true of iTunes Music Store?
   a it offers more tunes than Napster 2
   b it sold 14 million downloads in its first month
   c its success came as a surprise to the industry

2 Napster 2 is
   a a free file-sharing service.
   b only available on Apple computers.
   c an online pay per download service.

3 Sales of downloaded music are predicted to represent
   a 20 per cent of the global market.
   b six per cent of worldwide sales.
   c $7 billion every year.

4 The speaker thinks the music industry should
   a make file-sharers pay fines.
   b change their client base.
   c listen to their customers.

5 What mistakes has the music industry made in the past?
   a It hasn't spent enough on marketing.
   b It has ignored the importance of reality TV.
   c It has concentrated too much on short-term profit.

6 Which of the following should the music industry do?
   a increase the price of CDs
   b invest more in the right talent
   c spend less on big names like Eminem

Do you agree with what Gilles Philips has to say? What do you think the industry should do?

Giving reasons

Explaining why we make certain choices is part of everyday life. Look at the following expressions and decide which ones are more likely to be spoken and which ones are more commonly found in written English.

*The reason we want to reduce the price **is to** increase sales.*
*I want to do it that way **because** it's worked in the past.*
*The research was essential **in order to** check the validity of the theory.*
*I need to see him **so that** I can explain the problem in person.*
*The flight is delayed **due to** bad weather.*
***As** she's going to be late, we'll start the meeting without her.*
*It is a complex situation **given** the number of different factors to consider.*
***Since** it's raining, let's stay in for lunch.*

1 **Work in pairs. Match the situations with the reasons. Then write sentences using appropriate expressions.**

1	unfinished project	icy road conditions
2	the manager's bonus	so many people absent today
3	overtime started	long hours
4	train strike	backlog
5	late truck deliveries	wage cuts
6	meeting cancelled	unreasonable deadlines

2 **Give reasons why people do the following.**

1 download music from the internet
2 buy counterfeit brands of clothes
3 smoke
4 learn English
5 study Business

Showing feelings

Some cultures believe that showing passion and enthusiasm make an argument stronger. Others believe the strength of an argument relies on facts and figures and you should stay calm and in control. What about in your country? How might this difference cause misunderstanding in multicultural teams?

Dilemma & Decision

Dilemma: The Golden Couple™

Brief

Hollywood's golden couple, Catherine Zeta-Jones and Michael Douglas, sold the exclusive rights to their wedding photographs to the celebrity magazine *OK!* for £1m. Three days after *OK!* had published the 'exclusive' images, a rival celebrity magazine *Hello!* published an issue featuring pictures of the couple taken in secret at their wedding.

The couple decided to sue *Hello!* for intrusion of privacy for the sum of £50,000, comparing the distress of seeing the 'unflattering' photos to that of being burgled. They also sued for breach of commercial confidentiality, expecting, they said, £500,000 in compensation. The case raised the issue of how much control and trademark protection celebrities should have over their own image.

OK! magazine also filed a case against *Hello!* demanding damages of £1.75m to compensate for the disappointing sales of their 'exclusive' issue. As in all cases of this kind, the question of who would pay the legal costs, expected to be around £4.7m, would also have to be settled.

Task 1

Work in groups. Discuss the claims made by Zeta-Jones, Douglas and *OK!* magazine. Think about the following issues:

- Should the 'paparazzi' photograph celebrities without permission?
- Should celebrities be able to trademark their own faces?
- Should celebrities be protected from intrusion at private events?
- Do unauthorised photographs cause celebrities distress?
- Did *Hello!* have a right to publish the images taken in secret?

Task 2

Decide how much money, if any, you would award the Hollywood couple for each of the claims they are making. Then decide if *OK!* should be compensated by their rival and by how much. Finally, decide who should pay for all the legal costs.

Task 3

Present your decisions to the rest of the class and explain the reasons for your decisions.

Write it up

Write a short report of the points discussed and the recommendations made by your group. (See Style guide, page 26.)

Decision:

Turn to page 146 to find out what really happened when Catherine Zeta-Jones, Michael Douglas and *OK!* sued *Hello!* magazine.

Useful phrases

The reason ... is to ...
... so that ...
... in order to ...
... due to ...
... given the ...

The people's company

Keynotes

The **marketplace** brings together the buyers and sellers of goods and services and provides a framework for **negotiation** and **price setting**. The price at which goods and services are **exchanged** on a market fluctuates with **supply** – the quantity available for sale – and **demand** – the number of buyers. There are different types of markets which do not always have physical locations. Today, new **electronic marketplaces** have emerged on the internet where businesses can sell direct to consumers (**e-commerce**) or to other businesses (**B2B**). Some markets of this type use **auctions** where buyers submit **bids** and the highest bidder wins.

Types of markets

1 Look at the products below. Match the pictures with the kind of markets they represent.

1	commodities market	_____
2	real estate/property market	_____
3	stock market	_____
4	consumer goods/mass market	_____
5	labour market	_____

2 Think of one major item that you have either bought or sold recently. How did the transaction take place? Did you negotiate the price? Were you satisfied with the result?

3 Have you ever bought or sold something on the internet? What is different about buying things in an online market?

Electronic markets

1 Read the article about eBay – the online auction site. Which paragraphs A–F give information about the following things?

1	_____	what eBay does when it detects unusual activity by sellers
2	_____	possible threats to the developing business
3	_____	the different things you can buy on eBay
4	_____	how transactions are evaluated
5	_____	how popular eBay is
6	_____	why eBay conducts live interviews with buyers and sellers

2 Read the text again and answer the questions.

1 What conventional operating costs does the eBay model not have?
2 What services do the customers provide to the company?
3 How did eBay begin?
4 How is the company developing?
5 What are the main threats to eBay's future success?

Going, going, gone?

Will eBay's unique relationship with its customers become a casualty of the auction site's success?

A Meet the People's Company. Like a democracy, it can be a noisy place where citizens sometimes think the people in charge have no idea what they're doing. But at eBay, the online auction site, the people are in charge. Its customers – the 70 million buyers and sellers who trade here – have the kind of influence that most consumers and businesses can only dream of. It's true, eBay has a business model that doesn't require carrying any inventory. But the real secret of eBay's unlikely success is this: it's a master at capturing the awesome communications power of the internet, tracking customers' every movement so new products and services are tailored to just what they want.

B eBay's customers are its product development, market research, merchandising and sales department – all rolled into one. It's not just that they have made eBay into a global marketplace for almost anything, from a $1 baseball card to a $4.9m Gulfstream jet, eBay's customers also tell the world about eBay by word of mouth. They crowd online discussion boards, share tips, point out glitches, and lobby for changes. eBay's customers even police the site by rating each other. Imagine a retailer trying to do this: interview every single person leaving every store, post a list of what each thought of the shopping experience, ask them to write up a merchandising plan and call suppliers to arrange deliveries – and oh, by the way, could they keep an eye out for shoplifting? That's what eBay's customers voluntarily do each day.

C Back in 1995, when Pierre Omidyar unveiled Auction Web, he had much more in mind than simply helping his girlfriend trade Pez dispensers. He aimed to create a market for a wide range of goods, but with a difference. 'I wanted to give the power of the market back to individuals,' says Omidyar. But his biggest breakthrough was the Feedback Forum, a rating system that makes it easy for buyers and sellers to grade each transaction. Amazingly, it works. And positive ratings, which translate to more sales, keep people from going to other sites.

D Some of its most effective ways of getting user input, though, don't depend on the internet. Since early 1999, eBay has regularly flown in groups of sellers and buyers to its headquarters in California to interview them, asking for their views on new features and policies. The result: fewer problems. Even when something does go wrong, eBay can respond quickly. 'They can essentially negotiate with 50,000 users at once and make it work,' says Munjal Shah, CEO of Andale.

E Most of all, eBay simply watches. Almost all of its fastest-growing new categories grew out of observing seller activity. After noticing random car sales, eBay created a separate site called eBay Motors. This year, eBay expects to gross some $3.8bn worth of autos and parts – many of them sold by dealers. 'It's the way of the future,' says Bradley Bonifacius, internet manager at Dean Stallings Ford, Inc.

F eBay business is the company's latest offering; a new site providing businesses with an e-commerce platform. It's exciting new territory – and dangerous. Many rivals aim to be the biggest places for e-commerce, too, and some are making fast progress. But there's a bigger question. Can eBay's values survive such grand ambitions? Omidyar worries that the growing participation of large commercial sellers could dilute eBay's unique culture. 'If we lose that, we've pretty much lost everything,' he says. eBay's people power made building a business simple compared with everything conventional companies must do. Keeping in touch with all those customers from here on won't be easy.

Glossary

casualty someone hurt by events

awesome huge

tailored personalised

shoplifting theft from shops

dilute weaken

3 The following items were either sold on eBay or withdrawn from sale by eBay management. Guess which ones were actually sold and for how much. Turn to page 143 for the answers.

1 round of golf with Tiger Woods
2 missile silo house
3 woman selling herself for marriage
4 guest appearance on a TV show
5 square metre of land on a Scottish island
6 human kidney

Vocabulary 1 Complete the article with the following words.

> trading   auction   characteristics   business   inventory
> clients   rate   retailer

The essential guide to starting your own online business

If you are thinking of [1] *trading* on eBay then there are a few simple questions that you should ask yourself before you start. It's one thing to [2] _____ a few personal items from time to time but actually running your own online [3] _____ is a different thing altogether.

- What sort of product should you sell?
- What special [4] _____ does your product have that make it unique?
- How much [5] _____ will you need to stock to keep your [6] _____ supplied?
- How will customers [7] _____ transactions after a sale?

You can find the answers to all these questions and more in Kathleen Morton's new book *Online Business – The Easy Way*. Kathleen shares her secrets in this new book that could set you off on the road to becoming a successful online [8] _____ . Order now!

Vocabulary 2 ## Compound nouns

Match the two halves of the following compound nouns.

1 auction   a plan
2 merchandising   b site
3 feedback   c board
4 discussion   d platform
5 market   e forum
6 e-commerce   f research

Do the nouns refer to only online businesses such as eBay or conventional 'offline' businesses as well?

Gerunds and infinitives

Look at the following uses of the gerund.

- after prepositions
  *eBay's customers even police the site by **rating** each other.*

- as a noun
  ***Keeping** in touch with all those customers won't be easy.*

- after certain verbs
  *The eBay sellers enjoy **meeting** each other.*

Look at the following uses of the infinitive (*to* + verb).

- after adjectives
  *... makes it easy for buyers and sellers **to grade** each transaction.*

- after certain verbs
  *I wanted **to give** the power of the market back to individuals.*

- to show purpose
  *... flown in sellers and buyers to its headquarters **to interview** them, ...*

For more information and verb lists, see page 160.

Practice

1 **Complete the following profile of Pierre Omidyar, the founder of eBay, with appropriate gerund or infinitive forms.**

The world's most successful auctioneer

Pierre Omidyar is today at the head of one of the internet's biggest success stories: eBay. Born in France, Pierre moved to the USA at the age of six when his father was given the opportunity of ([1]work)___*working*___ at John Hopkins university. During his school years in the US Pierre started ([2]write)_____ computer programmes for six dollars an hour. ([3]Know)_____ how important computers would become in the future, he decided ([4]apply)_____ for a place at Tufts university. After ([5]graduate)_____ in 1988, Pierre then worked as a software developer before ([6]create)_____ his first start up 'Ink Development Corporation' in 1991. The company produced software that enabled computers ([7]read)_____ instructions given by pen and not through a keyboard. Five years later he succeeded in ([8]sell)_____ the company to Microsoft. It was not until 1995 that he came up with the idea of ([9]launch)_____ a website which would serve both as a market for ([10]exchange)_____ collectors' items and as a forum where collectors could meet ([11]discuss)_____ their passion. From a hobby it soon became a full-time occupation and after ([12]rename)_____ it eBay, the world's most open marketplace was born. Now a billionaire, Omidyar has set himself a new goal: ([13]get rid)_____ of 99 per cent of his fortune during his lifetime by ([14]finance)_____ non-profit-making operations around the world.

2 **Think of a non-profit-making project that you would support if you were Pierre Omidyar. Explain your ideas to your partner. Would he or she agree to donate money to your project?**

Making and responding to offers

From choosing restaurants to negotiating billion-dollar contracts, the same routine of suggestion and response happens in both business and everyday life. Look at the following ways of making suggestions.

What / How about ... ?

I think / suggest you / we should ...

Let's ...

Would you be interested in ... ?

Why don't I / you / we ... ?

Once one person has made a suggestion, the other person can either accept, refuse or ask for it to be modified. Which of the phrases below can be used to do each of these things?

1　*I'm afraid I / we can't ...*　　　refuse

2　*Maybe it would be better to ...*　_____

3　*OK. That's great.*　　　　　_____

4　*What / How about ... ?*　　　_____

5　*I don't know about that.*　　_____

6　*We could always ...*　　　　_____

7　*Done. / That's fine.*　　　　_____

8　*There's no way I / we can ...*　_____

Listening 1 ⊙

1 Listen to a short discussion. What are the speakers talking about? What is the outcome of their conversation?

⊙ **2** Listen again and complete the conversation with the phrases the speakers use.

At the moment we're doing a special offer on our top-of-the range laptops. Would you be interested?

Well, you know, they've only been on the market for a year and they're still retailing for £1,500. [2]_____ at ten per cent discount.

[4]_____ . How many would you need?

[6]_____ do that. You know they're worth more than that!

Well, I don't know about that. [8]_____ 13 per cent. I'll give you the warranty and you can pay half in advance and the rest in two months.

We'll see. [1]_____ discuss prices first.

There's no way we can afford that. [3]_____ _____ a better offer than that!

We'll need at least ten. [5]_____ 20 per cent off? We could work with that.

[7]_____ 15 per cent? And we'll pay you in three instalments. We'll also need a two-year warranty.

[9]_____ When can you deliver?

The selling process

1 Listen to Marsha Terrell, an e-commerce consultant, talk about how to advertise items online. What do each of the letters of AIDA stand for? Complete the notes.

Notes

A _____
I _____
D _____
A _____

Practice   **2** Look at the posting on an auction website. Does it follow the advice Marsha gives? Does it make you want to bid for the item?

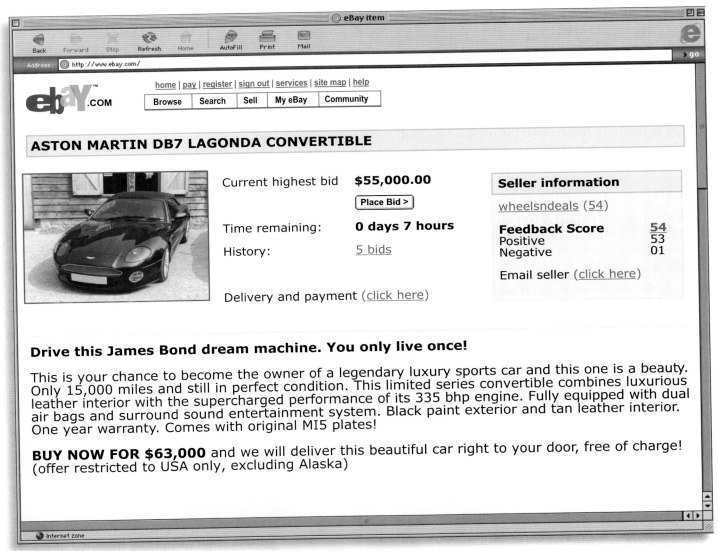

ebay .COM

home | pay | register | sign out | services | site map | help

| Browse | Search | Sell | My eBay | Community |

ASTON MARTIN DB7 LAGONDA CONVERTIBLE

Current highest bid   **$55,000.00**

Place Bid >

Time remaining: **0 days 7 hours**

History: 5 bids

Delivery and payment (click here)

Seller information

wheelsndeals (54)

Feedback Score   **54**
Positive   53
Negative   01

Email seller (click here)

Drive this James Bond dream machine. You only live once!

This is your chance to become the owner of a legendary luxury sports car and this one is a beauty. Only 15,000 miles and still in perfect condition. This limited series convertible combines luxurious leather interior with the supercharged performance of its 335 bhp engine. Fully equipped with dual air bags and surround sound entertainment system. Black paint exterior and tan leather interior. One year warranty. Comes with original MI5 plates!

BUY NOW FOR $63,000 and we will deliver this beautiful car right to your door, free of charge! (offer restricted to USA only, excluding Alaska)

Writing   Work in pairs. Choose a product that you would like to sell online. Prepare an advertisement to post on an auction website.

Culture at work   ## The importance of relationships

Some cultures prefer to build long-term business relationships and invest a lot of personal time socialising out of office hours to create trust and understanding. Other cultures prefer short-term relationships based on specific deals and contracts with little personal contact. What is common in your country?

Dilemma & Decision

Dilemma: Closing the deal

Brief

Watermark plc, is a specialist supplier of quality stationery and writing accessories, which it distributes in European markets. At present the sales of the company's leading products are not growing.

Hal Garnett, the newly appointed CEO, is in a hurry to reorganise the company's sales strategy and to introduce a new online sales channel. Since Watermark does not have the in-house expertise to develop such a site itself, it has decided to outsource the work.

Several web agencies have been contacted to obtain tenders to develop and maintain a new, eight-page site. Among the most interesting tenders that Watermark has received is from a new web agency called N-Vision. A meeting has been arranged with N-Vision to agree on the final specifications and budget for the new site.

Task 1

Work in goups. Group A you are the N-Vision representatives. Turn to page 142. Group B you are the Watermark sales team. Turn to page 138.

Task 2

Study the tender on page 141 and decide on your objectives for the meeting. What are you willing to compromise on?

Task 3

Prepare arguments to support your objectives. Make notes that you can refer to in the meeting.

> **Useful phrases**
>
> Why don't we ... ?
> Would you be interested in ... ?
> I'm afraid we can't ...
> I don't know about that.
> What / How about ... ?

Task 4

Work with a partner from the other group. Work together to reach a satisfactory agreement on the specifications in the tender. Present your arguments and try to achieve the best result for your company.

Write it up

Write a formal letter to the other company with minutes of the meeting and a summary of the agreement you reached. (See Style guide, page 16.)

Decision:

⊙ Listen to Andrew Harrison, an e-commerce consultant at Pryce & Hausman, explain what advice he would have given Watermark.

Unit 12
Lobbies

www.longman-elt.com   www.economist.com

Finding a voice

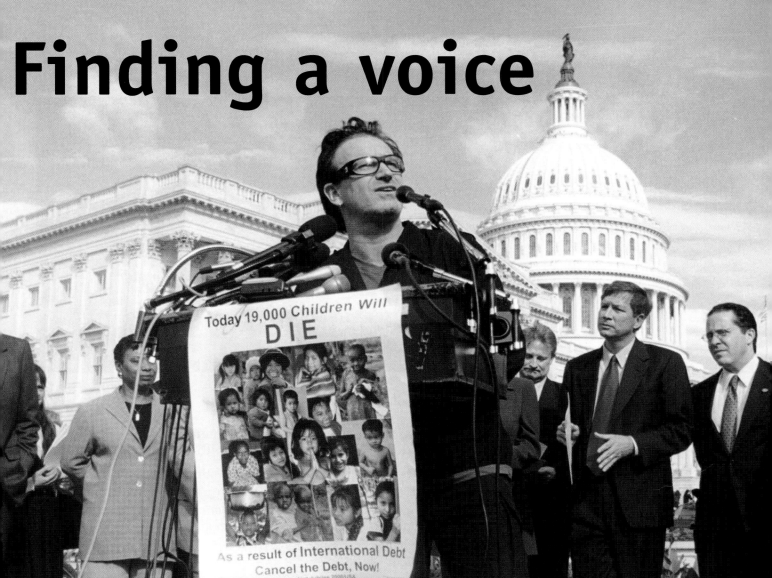

Today 19,000 Children Will DIE

As a result of International Debt
Cancel the Debt, Now!

Keynotes

Organisations such as **charities**, **pressure groups** and **industry groups** campaign or **lobby** governments or companies in an effort to persuade them to introduce or change policies. They can use any of the following methods to influence opinion: **demonstrations** – such as marches and sit-ins, **petitions** – collecting names and signatures on a letter of protest, **litigation** – taking legal action against companies or institutions, **boycotts** – refusing to buy products and services from a targeted company or **celebrities** to raise public awareness of a cause.

Acts of protest

Which of the following acts of protest would you be willing to take part in? Why? / Why not?

- demonstration against plans for a nuclear power plant near your home
- boycotting of clothes made by children in poor working conditions
- signing a petition against the killing of whales

Listening 1 ⊙ **Listen to three speakers describe successful protest campaigns and complete the table below.**

Who is being targeted?	
What do the protesters want?	
What method are they using?	

Reading **Fair trade**

Read the following sentences taken from the text on the opposite page. Then read the text and complete it with the sentences.

a Similar tactics helped to persuade the Bush administration to take a fresh look at foreign aid.

b Africa's share of world trade is a tiny two per cent, but the continent's exports are still ten times what it receives in aid.

c Europeans pay twice as much for a basket of groceries as do more liberal New Zealanders.

d Oxfam has just released a fat report on trade, in which it denounces rich countries' tariff barriers against imports from poor countries, and their subsidies for farmers.

e Bono spent two weeks touring Africa with Paul O'Neill, the US Treasury Secretary.

Speaking **Do you think celebrities should get involved in international politics and economics? Why? / Why not?**

Fair trade

Of celebrities, charity and trade

Charities are not yet free-traders, but some are halfway there

IN THE energy-sapping heat of Uganda, women bend double to grow flowers for export to Europe. According to Bono, singer of Irish rock band U2, this scene represents "globalisation at its best".

He is right, of course. Growing flowers is hard work, but no more so than subsistence farming, which is the alternative; and it pays better. Everyone benefits: Europeans get roses in winter and Ugandan rose-growers eat better and put their children through school. A number of organizations now recognise that trade between developed and less developed economies allows poorer countries to improve their economies. A number of charities have also noticed that north-south trade is not always exploitative. [1]_____. Another leading charity has condemned northern protectionism.

[2]_____ It was an odd spectacle: US finance ministers do not often spend time in African slums and rock stars rarely take part in high-level discussions about development economics. But the trip revealed a few things about the changing relationships between governments, charities and celebrities. Even

if politicians in democracies don't have to do what voters want, they generally do take their opinion seriously. So, if charities want them to be nice to Africa, they must persuade voters to demand this. And to attract voters' attention, it helps to have a few celebrities.

This tactic succeeded spectacularly during the "Jubilee 2000" campaign for debt relief. By using Bono and other famous people to draw attention to the problem, campaigners persuaded a record 25m people to sign their petition, which then pushed rich-country governments into cancelling a large part of poor-country debt. [3]_____ Mr O'Neill used to argue that aid was wasteful and created dependence; now he says that rich countries should give grants, not loans.

[4]_____ A small increase in trade would make far more difference than a proportionately similar rise in aid. Bono is not very clear about how this could be done, but DATA, the lobbying group he fronts, insists the rich world must lift quotas and duties on African exports, and cut subsidies that harm African growers.

That would be helpful. But there is also a selfish case for ending protection: that it would save taxpayers a fortune and make their food cheaper. [5]_____ The farm bill that George Bush signed is expected to cost the average US household $4,377 over the next decade. Poor Americans will suffer most, because they spend the largest share of their incomes on food. This continues partly because voters are unaware of it. "Fair trade" charities and their celebrities could surely stir a lot of people to angry protest over farm subsidies if they tried. But being charitable people they prefer to make liberalisation sound like the sacrifice it is not ■

Glossary

subsistence farming farming for food not trade

protectionism using tariffs to block imports

slum overcrowded and poor area of a city

Trade and lobbies

1 Put the words in the correct groups. Use a dictionary to help you.

fair trade   subsidies   celebrities   aid   tariff barriers   campaigners
duties   petition   exports   debt relief   imports   protectionism
charities   quotas

International trade	Lobbies

2 Now use some of the words to complete the text.

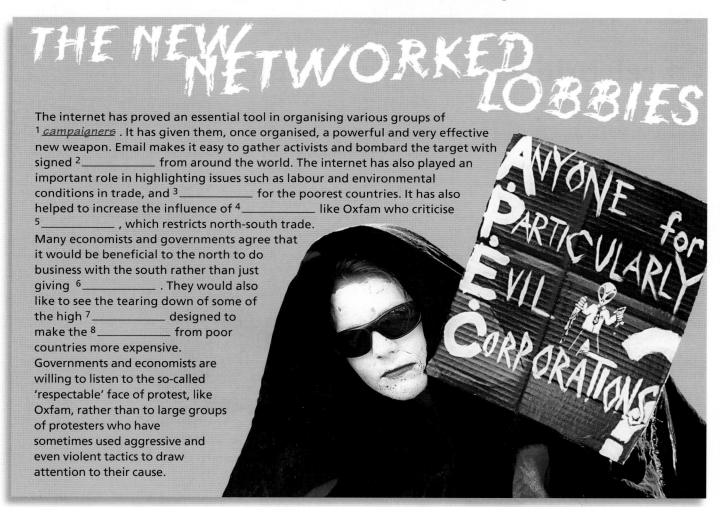

THE NEW NETWORKED LOBBIES

The internet has proved an essential tool in organising various groups of
[1] *campaigners* . It has given them, once organised, a powerful and very effective
new weapon. Email makes it easy to gather activists and bombard the target with
signed [2]_____ from around the world. The internet has also played an
important role in highlighting issues such as labour and environmental
conditions in trade, and [3]_____ for the poorest countries. It has also
helped to increase the influence of [4]_____ like Oxfam who criticise
[5]_____ , which restricts north-south trade.
Many economists and governments agree that
it would be beneficial to the north to do
business with the south rather than just
giving [6]_____ . They would also
like to see the tearing down of some of
the high [7]_____ designed to
make the [8]_____ from poor
countries more expensive.
Governments and economists are
willing to listen to the so-called
'respectable' face of protest, like
Oxfam, rather than to large groups
of protesters who have
sometimes used aggressive and
even violent tactics to draw
attention to their cause.

Speaking

Do you think internet petitions are a powerful and effective tool or
just junk mail? Have you ever signed one? Why? / Why not?

Modal verbs of obligation

1 **Look at the following sentences from the text. Which express:**

a   obligation, necessity or prohibition?

b   lack of obligation or prohibition?

c   advice or recommendation?

1   *Even if politicians in democracies* **don't have to** *do what voters want, they generally do take their opinion seriously.*

2   *... be nice to Africa, they* **must** *persuade voters to demand this.*

3   *... he says 'rich countries* **should** *give grants'.*

2 **Complete the table with the following verbs.**

have to   ought to   needn't   mustn't   shouldn't
need to   must   don't have to

obligation, necessity or prohibition				
lack of obligation or necessity				
advice or recommendation				

For more information, see page 159.

Practice   **Look at the statements from a UK charity, which donates computers to children in poor communities throughout the world and choose the best option to complete the sentences.**

1   There are many UK charities which provide computers to poor children in this country, so we feel we _____ worry about those children.
    a   ought to   b   need to   c   don't have to

2   We feel that we _____ concentrate our efforts in Africa.
    a   must   b   needn't   c   mustn't

3   We realise that we _____ just send computers to countries where there are no technology teachers.
    a   should   b   shouldn't   c   needn't

4   The children _____ learn how to use them as well.
    a   shouldn't   b   need to   c   mustn't

5   Therefore we _____ send teachers to some developing countries.
    a   have to   b   don't need to   c   shouldn't

6   If people wish to learn more about us they _____ visit our website.
    a   must   b   ought to   c   have to

Speaking   **What obligations affect you at work/school? Remember to make the difference between obligations and guidelines.**

Listening 2 Organising a campaign

Felicity Green is the press officer for a charity that takes care of elderly poor people. Listen to her talk about the importance of press coverage and complete the passages below.

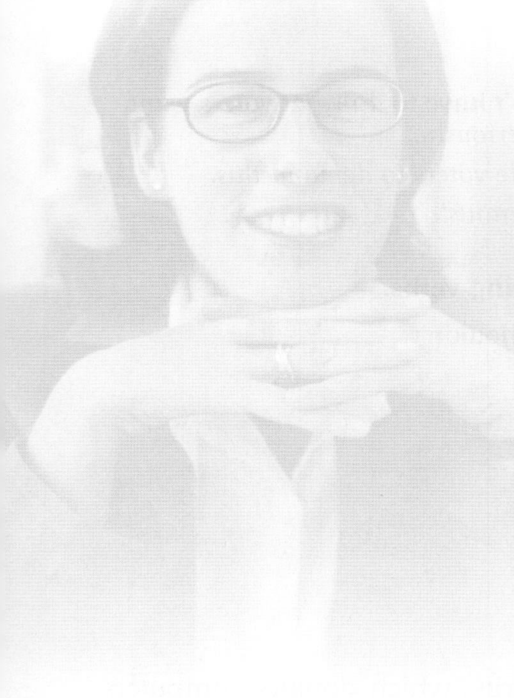

1 **What are the main objectives to have when planning a media campaign?**

a *Increase understanding*

b ____________

c ____________

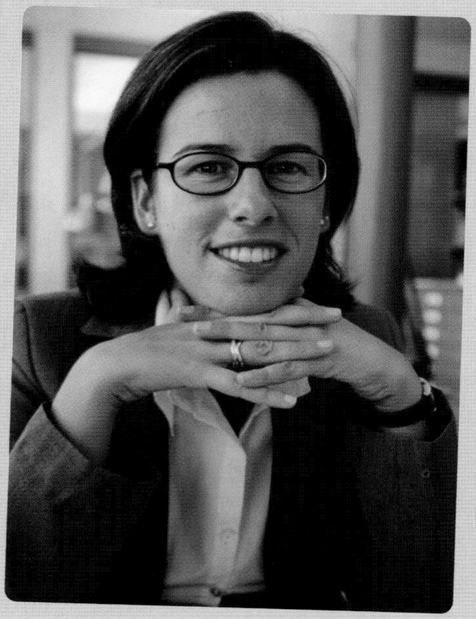

2 **What does the key message need to do?**

d ____________

e ____________

3 **What questions must you ask yourself when preparing a news release?**

f ____________

g ____________

h ____________

Vocabulary 2

1 **Felicity uses the following discourse markers to structure and clarify her ideas. Put these spoken words and phrases in the correct groups.**

firstly therefore also in order to let's say finally because then for example what's more and as you see so

1 showing sequence or order	
2 introducing new information	
3 linking cause and effect	
4 exemplifying a point	

2 **Would you use these discourse markers in formal letters or informal emails?**

Making a case

A good way to influence people's opinions is to find points they agree with and then build on these to make your case. Look at the following phrases for introducing ideas that you expect your listener to agree with.

It's obvious that ...   *You have to remember that ...*
We all know that ...   *Don't you think ... ?*
Have you considered ... ?   *Wouldn't you agree that ... ?*
I'm sure you must agree that ...   *Surely you can see ...*

Listening 3

1 **Listen to four short dialogues. Do you find the arguments effective? Rate them from 1–5 and explain why.**

argument   effectiveness (1–5)

1 _____   _____
2 _____   _____
3 _____   _____
4 _____   _____

2 **Listen again and tick the phrases you hear from the list above.**

Speaking

Work in pairs. Choose one of the topics below. Prepare arguments either for or against the topic chosen and present them to the class. Begin your argument with points you think the class will agree with.

– demonstrations are a waste of time
– corruption is inevitable in politics
– money is the only measure of success

Culture at work

Attitudes to silence during discussions

In some cultures, when one person stops speaking another will start straight away. In others it is a mark of respect to wait for silence until you start to speak. Whereas in other cultures, several people can all speak at the same time. How about in your country? What difficulties might these differences cause in multicultural meetings?

Dilemma & Decision

Dilemma: Selling up or selling out?

Brief

Milton S Hershey founded Hershey Foods, the USA's biggest chocolate maker, in 1903. Mr Hershey was a model employer who built a town for his employees with comfortable homes, inexpensive public transport and good schools. In 1909 he established a school for disadvantaged children. Many of the company's managers, including a former chief executive, are graduates from the school. In 1918 he gave the school his entire fortune of Hershey company shares. He put a board of trustees in charge of the school and its finances.

In July 2002 the school's trustees announced their plan to sell the chocolate factory to one of its competitors. Campaigners from the school, the company and former trust members joined residents of the Hershey town, to protest against the sale. They were also supported by the Pennsylvania state legal department. The board, who had never expected such a reaction, were faced with a serious dilemma. To sell or not to sell.

Task 1

Work in pairs. Student A you are a member of the trust. Turn to page 142. You are convinced of the sound financial reasons for selling. Student B you are a resident of Hershey. Turn to page 139. You want to persuade a trustee member that they should not sell the company.

Turn to page 142.
Turn to page 139.

> **Useful phrases**
>
> I take your point but ...
> Have you considered ... ?
> It's important you understand ...
> Have you taken into account ... ?
> I don't think you get the point that ...
> Don't you see ... ?

Task 2

Look at the information at the back of the book and prepare your arguments. Think what points the other person will agree with and build on these points to make your case.

Task 3

Discuss the case with your partner and try to reach a decision on whether or not the company should be sold.

Write it up

Write a formal letter to the local newspaper explaining what the board of trustees should do and why. (See Style guide, page 16.)

Decision:

Turn to page 146 to find out what decision the Hershey trustees reached and how *The Economist* reported it.

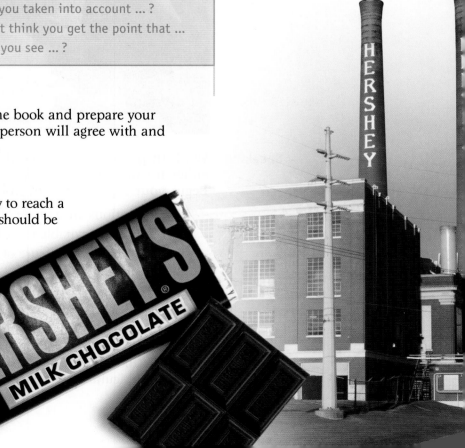

Review 4

Language check

Conditionals 1–3

Complete the sentences with the correct form of the verbs in brackets.

1 If I (find) _____ one on eBay, I (not / buy) _____ this, which probably costs twice as much as it should.

2 More consumers (shop) _____ on the internet if there (be) _____ better security.

3 If I (see) _____ the fake version, I (not / buy) _____ the genuine brand – but I didn't.

4 If electronic markets (not / exist) _____ consumers (have) _____ less choice.

5 If we (not / patent) _____ the design soon, someone else (do) _____ before us.

6 If you (want) _____ this meeting finished by three o'clock we (have) _____ to hurry.

7 The protest (not / be) _____ as effective if it (not / appear) _____ on the news tonight.

8 People (buy) _____ far more branded goods if they (not / be) _____ so expensive.

9 The supermarket (sell) _____ the grey imports if we (not / take) _____ legal action as quickly as we did.

10 If I (be) _____ you, I (not / buy) _____ a fake watch as you've no guarantee it will work.

Gerunds and infinitives

Complete the sentences below with the following verbs in the correct form.

organise   imagine   develop   come
save   help   buy   find

1 Would you consider _____ on a demonstration with me next weekend?

2 I offered _____ them finish the project but they refused.

3 _____ new markets is our main objective for next year.

4 The department head proposed _____ a meeting for tomorrow.

5 They are very interested in _____ our new range of products.

6 I hope _____ a job in Public Relations.

7 I got them on the internet, _____ money.

8 It's hard _____ a more efficient business model than eBay's.

Modal verbs of obligation

Which verb is the odd one out in each set?

1	must	should	have to	can
2	can	able to	must	allowed to
3	may	will	might	can
4	mustn't	can't	shouldn't	don't have to
5	ought to	need to	should	could

Consolidation

Underline the correct forms of the words in *italics*.

CAMPAIGNERS for urgent debt relief say that poor countries [1]*can / could* feed their children, if they [2]*didn't have / won't have* to pay huge sums of money back to wealthy countries in debt repayments. The money, originally borrowed in the 1970s and 1980s, was often badly invested instead of [3]*to be / being* used for worthwhile projects.

[4]*Repaying / To repay* the debt is going to be a huge millstone around the neck of the poorest countries who [5]*should / must* be concentrating their resources on sustainable projects. So who is this money they can't afford [6]*to pay / paying* back owed to?

The debts are mainly owed to two groups, Western governments and global financial institutions including the IMF and World Bank. They argue that if they [7]*cancelled / had cancelled* debt altogether, which is not the case, it [8]*would encourage / would have encouraged* wealthy countries to be against [9]*to lend / lending* and to insist on [10]*to cut / cutting* aid budgets. They also insist that they [11]*shouldn't / don't have to* be blamed for the debt problem.

But activists will never agree [12]*to stop / stopping* their campaign. They insist that most wealthy governments [13]*have had to / must* write off debts owed to them already as they know developing countries will simply never succeed in [14]*gathering / to gather* enough funds to pay off their debts.

Vocabulary check

1 Complete the text with the correct option A–C.

¹_____ of real brands or ²_____ goods in China are facing a smaller challenge than you might expect. Given that the country is one of the biggest and best producers of ³_____ and China's awful record on the protection of intellectual ⁴_____ rights, you might expect foreign ⁵_____ brand makers to stay well away.

However, the Swiss brand Omega is currently in ⁶_____ with China to set up shops in big hotels there. They expect the ⁷_____ for their products to be high, based on sales to Chinese people in Hong Kong.

Meanwhile, Western consumer ⁸_____ groups are calling on people to ⁹_____ cheap imports and copies from less developed economies due to growing concern about the working conditions of people who make them. ¹⁰_____ regularly gather outside these countries' embassies around the world in an effort to put pressure on governments to improve human rights conditions in their countries.

	A	B	C
1	A Merchandisers	B Dealers	C Sellers
2	A genuine	B valid	C proper
3	A fabrications	B fakes	C falsifications
4	A possessions	B property	C ownership
5	A luxury	B elegant	C classic
6	A chats	B discussions	C negotiations
7	A supply	B demand	C flow
8	A demonstration	B campaign	C pressure
9	A disapprove	B boycott	C dismiss
10	A Protesters	B Opponents	C Challengers

2 Complete the sentences below with the correct form of the following words.

demonstrate   forge   fraud   bribe   deceive

1 Appearances can be very _____ and sometimes fake products look like the real thing.

2 The police advised retailers that a large number of _____ €50 and €100 notes are in circulation.

3 A senior government official has been arrested and accused of seeking _____ from companies competing for government contracts.

4 The protesters are organising a major _____ in the city centre at the weekend.

5 Overcharging customers is a common example of _____ business activities.

Career skills

Giving reasons

Complete the sentences below with the following. Use each one only once.

so that   is to   because   as   given

1 The reason we want to take them to court _____ stop them counterfeiting our products.

2 Developed economies pay more than they should for food _____ of protectionist barriers against cheaper producing countries.

3 _____ they have many rivals, e-bay needs to keep a close eye on competitors.

4 Counterfeiting will be hard to stop _____ the profits to be gained from it.

5 We need to cancel the third world debt _____ they can feed their children.

Making and responding to proposals

Find and correct the mistake in each sentence.

1 I'm afraid I don't can make it tomorrow morning.

2 That's fine. I see you at five tomorrow.

3 We can meet as late on Monday how you want.

4 How about sometime on the afternoon?

5 That's great. Can five o'clock be OK?

6 I'm not sure. What time do you think of?

7 Would you be interesting in a 20 per cent discount?

8 There's not a way we can accept those terms.

Making a case

Match the sentence halves.

1 It's obvious that demonstrations ...

2 You have to remember that last time ...

3 I'm sure you agree that he ...

4 We all know the solution ...

5 Don't you think ...

a we should stop now and resume tomorrow?

b is to act now and get things done.

c is the obvious man for the job.

d do work, look at the success we've had so far.

e we had two extra weeks to complete the project.

Unit 13
Communication

www.longman-elt.com   www.economist.com

Messaging meltdown

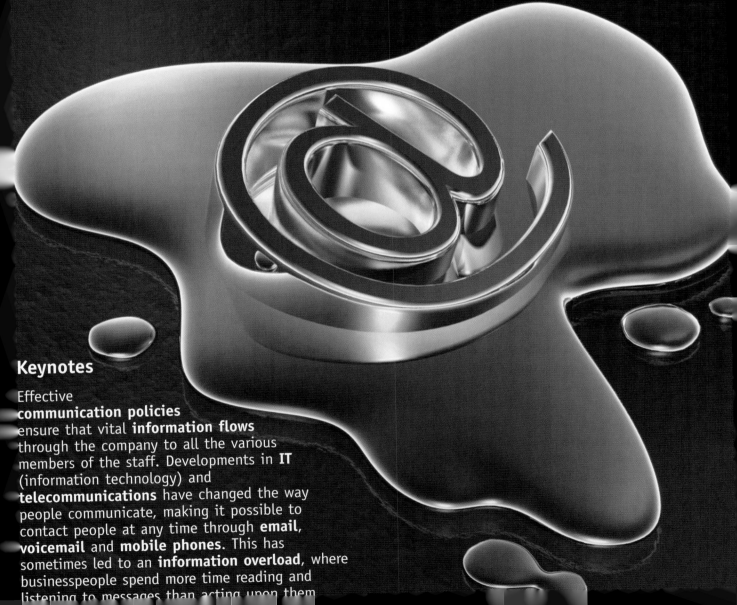

Keynotes

Effective **communication policies** ensure that vital **information flows** through the company to all the various members of the staff. Developments in **IT** (information technology) and **telecommunications** have changed the way people communicate, making it possible to contact people at any time through **email**, **voicemail** and **mobile phones**. This has sometimes led to an **information overload**, where businesspeople spend more time reading and listening to messages than acting upon them.

Let's communicate

1 What is your preferred way to communicate with friends and colleagues: email, telephone or text messaging? How much time do you spend talking on the phone, texting or sending emails?

2 Read the extracts sent to a human resources manager and say which type of business correspondence they come from. In what order would you respond to the messages?

A

For the attention of Ms Margaret Donnelly,
Human Resource Manager.

B

Hoping you will find the time to read my enclosed curriculum vitae.

C

As requested, our pricelist of preferential rates for conference bookings.
*Please note that to benefit from these prices, bookings for next month must be made before the end of this week at the latest.

D

Our top quality management courses can help you learn to prioritise and gain time.
*Places limited.
Phone 0800 355744 today!

E

All personnel who haven't collected their new security badges should do so before Friday this week, as the new system will come into effect from Monday morning.

F

To conclude, even though the project was completed on time, it came to my notice that key team members wasted far too much time dealing with paperwork and routine correspondence.

Reading **Information overload**

1 Read the text on the opposite page and identify how many of the above means of communication are mentioned. What other forms of communication are mentioned?

2 Match the following headings to each paragraph.

a   Making matters worse   _____

b   When in doubt, ask the boss   _____

c   A day in the life of an information junkie   _____

d   The causes of information overload   _____

e   The scale of the problem   _____

Information overload – *The ability to produce information is outstripping managers' ability to process it.*

Coping with infoglut

1 _____

If it isn't announced by a ring, beep, or flash, on your telephone it's delivered to your front desk by a person in a uniform. If it isn't spat out by a machine that looks like a printer but takes phone calls, it's transmitted to your PC, announced perhaps by a little toot of arrival. Welcome to the Age of Infoglut. Every day, managers are deluged by emails, faxes, post, voicemail. Just sorting everything out adds hours and extra stress to a working week. One British psychologist claims to have identified a new mental disorder caused by too much information; he calls it Information Fatigue Syndrome.

2 _____

Of course, companies have a huge appetite for information, and have encouraged the development of systems to produce, store, and analyse it. A recent study by Pitney Bowes, in Stamford, Connecticut, found that the average white-collar worker at a Fortune 1000 company sends and receives an average of 190 messages a day, in a variety of electronic and paper formats. 'It has become completely overwhelming,' says Sheryl Battles, executive director of external affairs at Pitney Bowes. She reported that trying to manage the volume of information was redefining productivity in the workplace. In a knowledge economy, the real goal is to get through all the messages. 'The infoglut has especially affected senior-level executives,' adds Battles. More than ever, managers need strategies for identifying and prioritising.

3 _____

Email is a primary culprit. In the past, lower-level workers would never have dreamed of interrupting the Chief Finance Officer with simple questions, such as whether hotel movies can be expensed. 'Today, however, those workers have no problem asking such questions via email, which is seen as less intrusive,' says Battles. It should be noted, however, that some executives have turned email to their advantage, finding in the medium a new and convenient way of running a business. Microsoft CEO Bill Gates, for instance, reportedly spends hours a day reading and sending email.

Glossary

deluge	large flood
overwhelming	too large to deal with
culprit	person guilty of a crime
junkie	addict

4 _____

The study also identified something Pitney Bowes calls messaging meltdown. That's when people try to reinforce their messages with other messages. For example, they might leave you a voicemail message that they are faxing a report. In addition, they might also send the report via email. Then, they might make a follow-up phone call to make sure you received the fax and the email.

5 _____

Arlen Henock, chief tax counsel at Pitney Bowes, didn't need a survey to find out which way the data is flowing. He said that there had been a significant increase over the last few years in his office. He also admitted that dealing with the flow has crept into his personal time. 'Each night I take home my faxes and other paperwork,' says Henock. During a typical workday Henock is a self-admitted information junkie. He gets up at 6 am and, over breakfast, finishes reading any paperwork left over from the night before. On the way to work he checks his voicemail with his car cell phone and responds to any messages that need immediate attention. 'Although I check my voicemail before I leave for home (typically at 7:30 pm), there are usually new messages in the morning,' he says. Europe, after all, has been up for hours.

3 **Read the text again. Are the following statements true or false?**

1   The new generation of computer printers can take phone calls.
2   New technology has increased office stress for managers.
3   Coping with information is now key to a manager's productivity.
4   Some managers find email to be an efficient way to get work done.
5   It is best to use a variety of means to communicate the same message.
6   Arlen Henock receives voicemail at night.

Speaking

What are the advantages and disadvantages of the following forms of communication?

post   email   fax   telephone   text messaging

Vocabulary

Information overload

1 **Choose the best option to replace the words in *italics*.**

1   Information is being produced faster than managers can *process* it.
   a   deal with   b   define   c   understand

2   Messages are *transmitted* to your PC throughout the day.
   a   received   b   dispatched   c   transformed

3   'It has become completely *overwhelming*,' says Sheryl Battles.
   a   wonderful   b   overpowering   c   overlooking

4   The average *white-collar worker* at a Fortune 1000 company sends and
   receives an average of 190 messages a day.
   a   manager   b   office worker   c   software technician

5   Email is seen as less *intrusive* than other forms of communication.
   a   personal   b   formal   c   disturbing

6   Email is a new and *convenient* way of running a business.
   a   fast   b   practical   c   instant

7   Bill Gates *reportedly spends* many hours a day reading and sending email.
   a   is said to spend   b   pretends to spend   c   enjoys spending

2 **Put the words in the correct groups.**

identify   prioritise   disorder   redefine   stress   analyse
interrupt   intrusive   store   fatigue   respond   manage

Negative effects of infoglut	Strategies for coping

Using email effectively

1 Charles Robinson lectures at major business conferences throughout the world on how to use email effectively. Listen to him talk about the advantages of email and complete the sentences.

Email:

1 Is _____ and _____ than snail mail.

2 Is less _____ than a phone call.

3 Is less _____ to use than a fax.

4 Means that differences in _____ and _____ are less an obstacle to information.

5 Leads to more _____ structures.

Writing

2 In part two Mr Robinson gives three useful tips on addressing emails. What are they?

Below is a summary of the other points Mr Robinson makes in his lectures. Read them and then write a reply to the email below.

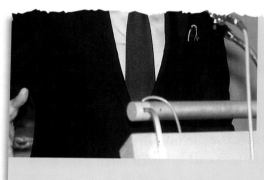

Tips on writing effective emails

Remember:

- Check you've given all the relevant information.

- Don't be too informal when writing to superiors or people outside the company, e.g. *Got your order, will give it to the guys at dispatches.*

- When answering emails use the reply button, this helps the receiver put your mail into context as the subject line will be repeated with 'RE' in front of it and the original message may be included.

- Never reply simply *yes* or *no* without repeating the context.

- Don't use pronouns out of context, e.g. I asked *them* and *they* agree.

From: Bill

subject: urgent: Monday task list

John
I know you're rushing off early today for the weekend but could you get back to me first thing Monday morning with the following information:
The date of the next meeting with the sales reps – I'd like to be there.

Your thoughts on your new assistant Miriam Anderson – are you happy with her?

Any recommendations for a salary increase or bonus for any of your team.
I'll be in the office early afternoon Monday but will be checking my mail from home. If you have any questions, contact me on my mobile from 8 am onwards.

Have a nice weekend
Bill

Reported speech

We can report what people say with direct speech (in inverted commas) or reported speech. Look at these examples and note the changes in tenses, pronouns, punctuation and word order.

1 *'It has become completely overwhelming,' says Sheryl Battles.*

2 *He said that there had been a significant increase over the last few years in his office.*

Now look at the following examples and complete the table.

example	direct speech		reported speech
1 'Why are you late?' He asked me why I was late.	*present simple*	$\rightarrow$	*past simple*
2 'We are trying to manage.' He said they were trying to manage.			
3 'I booked it last week.' He said he had booked it last week.			
4 'Have you been to Spain?' She asked if I'd been to Spain.			
5 'I won't be able to come.' She said she wouldn't be able to come.			
6 'We can come tomorrow.' They said they could come tomorrow.			

– Note: *would, could, should, might* and *ought* to stay the same.
   'She would love to meet you.' He thinks she would love to meet you.

– With orders, advice and requests we use the infinitive after the object.
   'Call me back later.' She asked him to call her back later.

 For more information, see page 161.

Listening 2 Listen to Jack Nelson's voicemail and complete the notes.
Take down essential details and then write up the notes for him.

MESSAGE FROM: Philip Jones   **TIME:** 8:15 pm
Called to say he was meeting José Dominquez for lunch at noon next
Tuesday at 'Chez Paul' and asked if you would like to go.

MESSAGE FROM: Mary Black   **TIME:** _____
Called to say she _____

MESSAGE FROM: Jean-Paul Cartier   **TIME:** _____
Said _____

MESSAGE FROM: Nigel Banks   **TIME:** _____
Asked if _____

MESSAGE FROM: Mr José Dominquez   **TIME:** _____
Explained that _____

MESSAGE FROM: Mary Black   **TIME:** _____
Called again and said _____

Summarising

The ability to pass on business information to colleagues about meetings, presentations and conversations they missed is an essential part of the information flow within a company. Sharing news about colleagues and the company (gossip) is also an important part of office life. Look at the following ways of summarising information you might wish to pass on.

What she was trying to say was ...
He was going on/talking about ...
Basically, what she said was ...
The important point is ...
The main thing is ...
He reckons/thinks that ...
The thing was ...
He told me that ...

Listening 3 Listen to five conversations. What is being talked about and which of the above phrases are used?

subject	phrases
1	
2	
3	
4	
5	

Speaking Work in groups. One person from each group write a piece of gossip and give it to the teacher. Then whisper the gossip to the next person in the group who in turn passes it on. The last person in the group should say aloud what they heard. Compare this to the written pieces of gossip.

Culture at work ## Attitudes to interruptions

In some cultures people like to focus on one thing at a time and dislike being interrupted during work and meetings. Other cultures tolerate disruptions such as phone calls during meetings and are happy to do several tasks at once. How might this difference cause misunderstanding in multicultural teams?

Dilemma & Decision

Dilemma: Spinning the truth

Brief

PR Vision is a communication agency that specialises in protecting reputations and corporate image in a time of media crisis. Their company motto is 'When dealing with the media, whoever tells the best story wins.' PR Vision has helped companies to successfully handle news stories about product recalls, job losses and scandals by responding in the press with news stories of their own which:

- quickly address issues and recognise when the company is at fault
- tell the truth and underline the positive action being taken
- look to turn crisis into an opportunity to produce positive publicity

Task 1

Work in groups. You will find newspaper cuttings about five of PR Vision's current clients on page 144. Read them and discuss the possible courses of action that each of the companies involved could take.

Task 2

Choose one client company to write a press release about. Use the following information to help you:

- introduce the company and say something positive about it
- acknowledge the problem (quote from company)
- outline what they propose to do about the dilemma
- finish on a positive note (e.g. give details of a future project)

Task 3

Prepare a draft of your press release. (See Style guide, page 30.) Check for mistakes and make sure it will have the right effect on the public.

Task 4

Listen to the other press releases in the class. Which group has spun the best story?

Useful phrases

It has been reported that ...
The important point is ...
The company has said / admitted ...
Our client says ...
The company has promised ...

Decision:

Turn to page 146 to see an example of a PR Vision News story.

The invisible industry

Keynotes

Logistics is the management of the **flow of products** from **raw materials** to finished goods. Smart logistics allow companies to reduce the costly **inventory** problem of overstocking. Thanks to improvements in the **freight industry** (road haulage, rail freight, shipping or air-cargo) as well as the international '**consolidators**' or '**integrators**' such as FedEx, UPS and Deutsche Post World Net, goods are moved ever more quickly and efficiently along the **supply chain**.

Demand and supply

Discuss the following questions in pairs.

1 Have you ever gone to the shops to buy something and not been able to find it? If so, how did you react?

2 Why do shops not always have all their usual stock?

3 Even goods that make it to the shelves can disappear because of theft. How do retailers try to reduce this problem?

Reading **Retail logistics**

1 Read the text on the opposite page about 'smart tags'. List the four advantages of using smart tags that are mentioned.

2 Choose the best option to answer each of the questions.

1 According to the text which of the following is going to happen?
   a smart tags will reduce sales of consumer goods
   b the cost of smart tags will run into tens of billions of dollars
   c supermarket staff will be alerted when goods are stolen

2 Traditional Radio Frequency Identification was
   a less efficient than the new smart tags.
   b harder to produce than the new smart tags.
   c more expensive than the new smart tags.

3 Gillette's experiment will
   a cost $30 billion.
   b tag shelves as well as goods.
   c use barcodes to track goods.

4 Using smart tags to monitor products will
   a reduce the number of mistakes usually made.
   b increase the quantities of goods shipped.
   c increase the number of inventories.

5 By using the 'kill command' consumers will
   a lose their privacy.
   b receive after-sales benefits.
   c lose after-sales services.

Speaking **Would you object to buying goods with smart tags? Why? / Why not?**

Glossary

adoption mass use of something

shrink make smaller

invasive entering without permission

forego decide not to have something

Retail logistics

The best thing since the barcode

Smart labels may be about to change the way that companies distribute and sell almost everything they make.

AT A Tesco's supermarket in Cambridge, England, the shelves have begun to talk to their contents, and the contents are talking back. Soon, razors at a Wal-Mart store in Brockton, Massachusetts will begin to let staff know when they suspect theft. A group of firms will attempt to track, in real time, many thousands of goods as they travel from factory to supermarket shelf. Consultants talk about cost savings and extra sales that could run into tens of billions of dollars a year.

The reason for the sudden excitement is a new, super-cheap version of an old tracking technology called Radio Frequency Identification (RFID). RFID systems are made up of readers and "smart tags" – microchips attached to antennas. When the tag nears a reader, it broadcasts the information contained in its chip. In the past four years the cost of the cheapest tags has plunged from $2 to 20 cents. In the next two to three years prices are likely to fall to five cents or less. Gillette announced that it had put in an order for half a billion smart tags, signalling the start of

their adoption by the consumer goods industry. If they catch on, smart tags will soon be made in their trillions and will replace the barcode on the packaging of almost everything that consumer goods giants such as Procter & Gamble and Unilever make.

Gillette is piloting two uses for its tags. The first combines smart tags with "smart shelves", which are fitted with tag readers. Gillette says that retailers and consumer goods firms in the USA lose around $30 billion a year in sales because shop shelves run out of products and stand empty. On Gillette's smart shelves, the tagged razors let the shelf know when they are coming and going, and the shelf keeps count. If it gets too empty, the shelf sends a message to store staff to say it needs to be filled.

Gillette is also piloting the use of smart tags to track products as they move from factory to supermarket. Using barcodes can be a labour-intensive, error-prone task. Smart tags can be scanned automatically as pallets of products pass along conveyor belts and through loading bays. As a result, ship-

ment errors and theft will be reduced, argues Gillette. Because manufacturers can be certain that they are shipping the right quantity of goods to the right place at the right time, they can also afford to shrink the inventories they maintain in case of error.

The biggest worry is that consumers might reject smart tags because they seem too invasive of their privacy. If firms link products to customers at the checkout, ordinary objects could become traceable to their purchasers (imagine a stray drinks can at the scene of a crime). Here too the Auto-ID Centre seems ahead of the game. Its chip specifications include a "kill command" that can permanently disable the tag. The centre is working on a privacy policy, a draft of which gives the customer the option to kill tags at the checkout. The customer would forego after-sales benefits, such as better warranty and returned goods services, for instance, or chickens that could tell ovens how to cook them. But the kill command is just the thing for those who suspect that their fridge has begun to spy on them ■

Supply chain management

Put the words and phrases in the correct groups.

run out of   keep count   broadcast   antennas   microchips
empty shelves   store staff   scan readers   fill   disable/kill

inventory control	smart tag technology

Compound nouns

Match the words to form word partnerships.

1	after-sales	a	belt
2	returned goods	b	benefits
3	error-prone	c	bay
4	conveyor	d	versions
5	loading	e	task
6	super-cheap	f	industry
7	consumer goods	g	service

Now use the word partnerships to complete the sentences.

1 Most electronic products carry a warranty and *after-sales benefits* .

2 Accounting software has greatly improved the _____ of having to come up with exact figures.

3 Goods are put onto lorries at the factory _____ .

4 When supplies arrive at the factory they are placed on a _____ to be transported straight to the workshops.

5 Fake goods are usually _____ of expensive brands.

6 The _____ is interested in the new tracking technology.

7 Our _____ is expensive to run but customers really appreciate being able to bring things back if they need to.

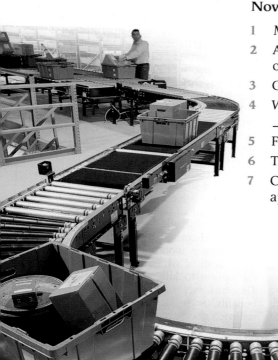

Word-building

Complete the table with the correct form of words from the text on page 121.

	verb	noun
1	*distribute*	distribution
2		excitement
3	broadcast	
4		adoption
5	combine	
6		shipment

The smart tag press conference

1 Kate Upshaw, a retail specialist, talks about the advantages smart tags will offer retailers and manufacturers. Listen to part one and note the points she makes.

2 In part two Kate deals with questions from journalists. Put the following topics in the order they are discussed.

security mistakes privacy unemployment

	Topic	Response
1		
2		
3		
4		

Now listen to part two again. Does Kate actually answer each question? Make notes on her responses.

3 In part three one of the journalists talks about measures retailers should take to protect consumers. Listen and make notes.

1 _____
2 _____
3 _____

Speaking

Do you think the measures the journalist mentions would work? Why? / Why not? Would you mind companies monitoring your movements?

Passives

The passive is formed with the appropriate tense of the verb *be* + the past participle of the main verb.

... *smart shelves which* **are fitted** *with tag readers.*

Smart tags **can be scanned** *automatically.*

As a result, shipment errors and theft **will be reduced.**

– We use the passive form when the agent is unimportant.

The tags **are** *currently* **being piloted** *in major supermarkets (by Gillette).*

– The passive is often used in formal reports and notices.

It **has been established** *that shipment errors* **will be** *greatly* **reduced.**

For more information, see page 161.

Practice

1 **Write the following sentences in the passive. Do not include the agent if it is not important.**

1 Consumer groups have brought the issue of consumer privacy to light.
   The issue of consumer privacy has been brought to light.

2 Manufacturers will install smart tags on all sorts of products.
   _____

3 Consumer groups are preparing petitions against the use of smart tags.
   _____

4 Lorries and trucks transport raw materials to the factories.
   _____

5 Supermarkets are considering eliminating checkouts altogether.
   _____

6 Consumers should try to access more information about smart tags.
   _____

2 **Complete the text with either the appropriate active or passive form of the following verbs.**

make   find   buy   load   use   scan   track   remove   access
send   transport   insert   throw away

During one of the last stages of production, tag readers ¹ *are inserted* into the packaging of certain items destined for a well-known supermarket chain.

They are then ² _____ onto trucks and ³ _____ to the supermarkets.

A young woman ⁴ _____ one of these items and ⁵ _____ her credit card to pay for it. Information about her, such as her name, address and a list of all the items in her shopping trolley ⁶ _____ into the shop's computer system.

She then ⁷ _____ various purchases in different stores, paying each time with the same credit card.

What she doesn't realise is that all her movements ⁸ _____ and that until the packaging of the tagged item ⁹ _____ and ¹⁰ _____ information about everywhere she goes, everything she buys and how much she is willing to pay for items ¹¹ _____ easily by marketers and retailers.

Soon, a letter ¹² _____ to her suggesting that all the products she prefers to buy from high street retailers ¹³ _____ in the supermarket at more competitive prices.

Dealing with questions

In situations such as job interviews, dealing with clients, meetings and giving presentations, the ability to deal with difficult questions is very useful. There are different reasons why questions might be considered difficult. For example, the person

a   doesn't know the answer.
b   knows the answer but doesn't want to tell the truth.
c   knows the answer but finds the question inappropriate.

1 **Look at these questions and decide why they might be difficult (a–c above). In what situations might they be asked?**

1   Why did you leave your last job?
2   How do you react to criticism?
3   The figures don't make sense. Where did you get them from?
4   So, how much do you earn?
5   You say the sales are up ten per cent. Can we have a breakdown, please?
6   I still haven't received my order. What's going on?

Dealing with difficult questions requires answers that:

a   buy time
b   have been carefully prepared to make a good impression
c   repeat positive messages to avoid direct answers
d   avoid answering by asking another question

Listen to six people deal with difficult questions. Which strategies are used? Some answers combine more than one strategy.

Work in groups. Prepare difficult questions to ask other groups about the following topics. Then practise asking and answering the questions with another group.

the company   the economy   your teacher   a bad sporting performance

Attitudes to critical questions

In some cultures any form of questioning or criticism in public is very impolite. In other cultures it is important to speak out and criticism is not taken personally. What is common in your culture? How might this difference cause misunderstanding in multicultural teams?

Dilemma & Decision

Dilemma: Is grey the new black?

Brief

Many producers of branded goods refuse to distribute through supermarket chains, fearing that price-cutting could damage their brand image. They distribute exclusively through selected retailers. Grey marketers challenge this by obtaining branded goods through alternative supply routes and selling them at much cheaper prices.

Best Value is a leading UK supermarket chain that has been offered a 'grey consignment' of genuine branded jeans at a very heavily discounted price. The brand-owner, GenX, is aware of the situation and has threatened legal action if Best Value sells the jeans. Best Value could sell a lot of the jeans and even the legal threats from GenX could generate positive publicity. However, losing a major legal battle could be costly and sales of Best Value's own brand of jeans could suffer.

Task 1

Work in groups. You are Best Value's purchasing team. Look at the information below. List the advantages and disadvantages of accepting the consignment of GenX 250 jeans.

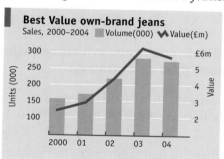

Best Value own-brand jeans
Sales, 2000–2004 ■ Volume(000) ◆ Value(£m)

GenX 250 sales forecast
(UK High Street price = £45)

Task 2

Discuss the best course of action to take. Possible options include:

1 Refuse the GenX 250 jeans.

2 Sell the jeans but hope to get GenX's permission by negotiating an acceptably high retail selling price.

3 Accept the shipment and sell the jeans at the heavily discounted price risking legal action from the brand-owner.

Task 3

Each group presents its decision to the rest of the class. The other groups should ask questions about the proposed action.

Write it up

Write a formal fax to GenX explaining what course of action you are going to take and why. (See Style guide, page 20.)

Decision:

Turn to page 146 to find out what happened to Tesco, a UK supermarket chain, when it was in a similar situation.

Pushing the limits

Keynotes

Innovation has become a critical factor for commercial success. Businesses can innovate in a number of different ways; by launching products with **new features**, by providing improvements to existing services, by introducing more **effective business practices** and by finding new markets and sources of supply. **Launching an innovation** involves a **degree of risk** but, if successful, an entrepreneur can produce better **returns** as **margins** will be high especially when competitors' products become **obsolete** as a result.

Product development

1 Look at these products that were revolutionary when first introduced. How have these products been developed over time? What new features and designs have improved their quality?

2 How creative are you? Answer the following questions and check your score on page 137.

		Never	Sometimes	Always
1	I look for solutions to difficult problems.	☐	☐	☐
2	I see things that other people don't notice.	☐	☐	☐
3	I like to find ways to connect different things together.	☐	☐	☐
4	I note down interesting ideas as they come to me.	☐	☐	☐
5	I don't always respect decisions made by those in authority.	☐	☐	☐
6	I like to keep myself informed about new developments.	☐	☐	☐
7	I like taking risks.	☐	☐	☐
8	I am perseverant.	☐	☐	☐
9	I will take unpopular positions if I think I am right.	☐	☐	☐
10	I like to discuss things with other people.	☐	☐	☐
	Points	0	1	2

Mastering design

1 Look at the sample designs produced by the Alessi factory in Italy. What do you think of them?

2 Now read the article on the opposite page. Are the following statements about Alberto Alessi true or false? Correct the statements.

1 He is the only member of his family to work for the company.
2 The company has always been owned by the Alessi family.
3 He wants his firm to design only household objects.
4 He designed the famous Bird Kettle.
5 All his designers are company employees.
6 He doesn't mind talking about products that have failed.
7 He supervises the planning of new projects.
8 More than half of his new products fail.

Alberto Alessi transformed his family's housewares business into a trendsetting design giant. His secret: walking the borderline between genius and failure.

Has your latest project bombed? There's only one thing to do, says Alberto Alessi, godfather of Italian product design: Revel in your glorious failures. Dance on the borderline between success and disaster. Because that's where your next big breakthrough will come from.

Alessi, 54, has followed that very advice ever since he took the reins of the family business in 1970. His partnerships with some of the world's best designers have transformed this 80-year-old company from housewares supplier to design leader. You might not know them as Alessi offerings, but most people can recognise Philippe Starck's Juicy Salif lemon squeezer and Michael Graves's Bird Kettle.

But Alessi is just as proud of his flops. It's the duds that enjoy centre stage in the company's private museum, where Alessi's designers meet weekly to discuss new projects. He has even published a book of prototypes that never made it to production. In a market that's crowded with the mundane and generic, Alessi says, the lemons reassure him that he is not veering toward safety.

Fortunately, most of the products created by Alessi's impressive stable of 200 free-agent designers are winners. The Alessi 'dream factory' of 500 workers, which Alberto runs with brothers Michele and Alessio, has over the past decade raised sales by around 15 per cent a year, to $100 million today.

Now, having conquered our kitchens, Alessi is looking at our cell phones, watches and maybe even our cars. How will he do it? By walking along the border between the 'possible and the not possible.' In an interview at the Alessi factory he explained how to fail in style.

Where is this borderline?

The area of the 'possible' is the area in which we develop products that the customer will love and buy. The area of the 'not possible' is represented by the new projects that people are not yet ready to understand or accept. At Alessi, we work as close as we can to the borderline. Because when we succeed, we give birth to a new product that surprises people and because it is completely unknown, it doesn't have any competition — which means we can enjoy big margins.

How do you explain your success?

Our industrial organisation is very flexible. We have a few best-sellers that sell more than 100,000 pieces a year, while others sell in much smaller numbers. In any case, Alessi is not a mass-production company. It's a research lab for the applied arts. And that means we have to experiment a lot. But doing experiments doesn't just mean doing the research and making a prototype. It means putting a finished product into the marketplace.

What is your favourite fiasco?

Our most beautiful fiasco was the Philippe Starck Hot Bertaa kettle. I didn't realise that we had gone too far. Inside the kettle was some complicated but very intelligent engineering. On the prototypes, it worked well, but when we produced thousands and thousands, it didn't work so well.

How do you view your customers?

Our customers seem happy to take risks with us. Customers are much more progressive than marketing people or retailers think. Society is much more exciting than just a target market. A target market is a cage where people try to put society. It bears no relation to what people feel and want.

Failure is glorious

Synonyms

Put the following words and phrases into five groups of synonyms. Use a dictionary to help you.

failures   devise   boundary   achievement   duds   frontier   brink
disaster   accomplishment   dream up   lemons   advance   success
fiasco   invent   adapt   alter   revamp   change   threshold   edge
think up   modify   flops   come up with

Product development

1 The process of developing new products can be divided into different phases. Put the following phases in the correct order.

business analysis   manufacturing   development   imagining   launch

2 Now match the following tasks with the five phases.

a   deliver to distributors
b   troubleshooting
c   brainstorming
d   build a prototype
e   promote the product

f   predict sales volume
g   organise production
h   quality control (QC)
i   evaluate costs

3 Complete the chart below with the following quotes.

a   Certification delayed
b   Nothing like it on the market
c   Problems with QC
d   Production back on schedule
e   Distributor gets stock

f   Find cheaper suppliers
g   Back to the drawing board
h   Boss says it's too expensive
i   We have an idea!
j   Profit study looking good

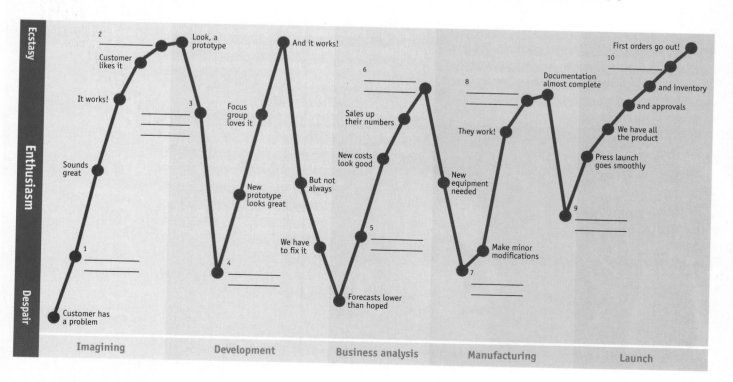

Work in pairs. Think of as many examples as possible of products that were genuinely innovative when they were launched. How many of these have you bought or used yourself?

Great innovators

1 Listen to Julie Reynolds, of *Design Magazine*, talk about two famous British designers – Jonathan Ive and Trevor Bayliss – and match the designers to the following products.

2 Listen to Julie again and answer the following questions.

1   After graduating, Jonathan Ive went to work at
   a   the Design Museum.
   b   Tangerine.
   c   Apple Computer.

2   His first design for Apple Computer was a
   a   desktop computer.
   b   portable music player.
   c   laptop computer.

3   Ive's revolutionary designs have
   a   increased Apple's sales.
   b   transformed the image of computers.
   c   created new markets for Apple.

4   After leaving the army Bayliss
   a   designed swimming pools.
   b   became a professional sportsman.
   c   worked as a salesman.

5   Bayliss's main achievement has been to
   a   make modern technology available everywhere.
   b   improve economic conditions in poor countries.
   c   make products affordable to everyone.

What effect do you think the work of Ive and Bayliss has had? What other innovators have changed the way we think and live?

When we talk about the past we often refer to hypothetical events and situations. For example, when we want to:

- talk about alternative possibilities in the past

  With more time we **could have improved** *the design.*

- give advice after events have happened

  She **should have patented** *the process immediately.*

- talk about likelihood in the past

  I **may have made** *a mistake in the calculations.*

Past modals are formed with: modal verb + *have* + past participle.

 For more information, see page 159.

| Practice | **Read the description of a failed innovation. Complete the statements below with the appropriate past modal forms of the following verbs.**

research   design   waste   stop   know   charge
conduct   miscalculate   spend

Motorola and Iridium

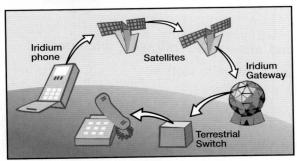

The Motorola Iridium satellite network

IRIDIUM WAS MOTOROLA'S grand design for a communications network that would include dozens of orbiting satellites and allow people to communicate through handsets from anywhere in the world. The project was extremely complex and took more than ten years to develop at a cost of over $5bn. Customers had to buy Iridium handheld phones at a cost of $3,000 and pay between $3 and $5 per minute for calls. The handsets were heavy and some people complained that they didn't work inside buildings and cars. Iridium never made a profit and by 1999 had gone bankrupt after failing to generate more than 55,000 subscribers – not enough even to pay the interest on the money the company had borrowed. In the meantime mobile phones had appeared on the market.

1   They <u>*should have researched*</u> the technology more thoroughly.
2   They _____ money developing their own systems.
3   They _____ the system was going to be too expensive.
4   They _____ the project before it was too late.
5   They _____ lighter handsets.
6   They _____ less for calls.
7   They _____ a more successful marketing campaign.
8   They _____ so much time and energy.
9   They _____ the size of the potential market.

| Speaking | **Work in pairs. Think of a decision you made in the past which may not have been the best one in the circumstances. Tell your partner what happened and say how you should / could have acted instead.**

Reviewing achievement

Identifying areas where individual performance can be improved provides an opportunity for learning and improvement. Giving feedback to other people is difficult as badly phrased comments can be seen as criticisms. Which of these phrases congratulate someone on what they have done and which encourage them to improve their performance?

I'm really impressed.
I'm a little disappointed.
You've done a fantastic job.
How come you weren't able to ... ?
Don't you think it would have been better if you'd ... ?
Couldn't you have ... ?
I don't think you should have ...
No one could have done a better job.

Listening 2 ⊙ **Listen to three conversations where people discuss achievement. In which of the conversations is one of the speakers:**

– praising
– pointing out some minor weaknesses
– giving negative feedback

Practice **1 Often, the hardest performance to review is your own. Think of a group project or activity you have been part of recently and use the following questions to assess your own performance.**

– How did my strengths contribute to the team as a whole?
– What were my weaknesses?
– How did my weaknesses slow down the work of the team?
– Is my present work satisfactory or do I need to review my methods?
– What lessons did I learn from this for the future?
– What motivated and inspired me most?

2 Working in pairs. Take it in turns to interview each other about the project your partner has chosen. Find out what you think you can each learn from your experiences.

Culture at work **Giving praise**

In some cultures people are praised and rewarded for their individual performance. In other cultures being singled out is very embarrassing and praise should be given to a whole group or team who worked together. What is common in your culture? How might this difference cause misunderstanding in multicultural teams?

Dilemma: Prize pitch

Brief

TechStart is a European business association that promotes emerging technology and new business ventures. Originally founded to help young university graduates to gain access to funds, TechStart today offers future entrepreneurs a comprehensive one-year programme of assistance, advice and training in order to turn creative new ideas into fully operational business ventures. Every year TechStart organises a competition where graduates can submit their proposals for new business ventures. The winning project team receives a cash prize of 50,000 and joins the one year StartUp Programme. During this year the new business is offered free office space, access to research facilities, business management training and support from one of the universities participating in the programme.

These four projects have reached the final. Each project team is to make a short presentation to the competition jury. (Project details on page 145.)

1. ZephGen: Wind-powered electricity scheme.
2. Rainbow Systems: Heat-sensitive packing materials.
3. Open Tour: Mobile phone tourist guide service.
4. VoxData: Mood recognition software for customer services.

Task 1

Work in small groups. Choose one of the projects and make notes about the following:

1. an outline of what your project is
2. the main features of your product
3. who will benefit from your product and how
4. how you will use the prize should you win it

> **Useful Phrases**
>
> You might have considered ...
> You've done a fantastic job ...
> You could have ...
> We were really impressed by ...

Task 2

Organise your ideas into a short presentation. Practise giving the presentation and make any necessary changes to improve it.

Task 3

Present your project to the class.

Write it up

Listen to the other groups and choose the best presentation. Then imagine you are a member of the jury and write a letter to the winning group giving them feedback on their project and presentation. (See Style guide, p16.)

Decision:

- Listen to Candy McQuire, an expert in new business ventures, talk about how she would evaluate the presentations.

Review 5

Language check

Reported speech

Rewrite the following sentences in reported speech.

1 Can you find solutions to difficult problems?
   He asked me _____ .

2 I'm looking for ways to improve IT support.
   She told me _____ .

3 I'll take unpopular positions when necessary.
   I told him _____ .

4 The thing we hated most was the stress.
   They said _____ .

5 I saw something no one else noticed.
   I explained _____ .

6 I won't be able to come.
   He rang to say he _____ .

Passives

Write the following sentences in the passive. Don't include the agent if it isn't important.

1 My assistant sorts all my mail in order of priority.
   _____

2 You have to take risks in a business like this one.
   _____

3 Last year we sent over 1,000 email messages a day.
   _____

4 You should only use one means of communication per message.
   _____

5 They've held discussions on the subject of privacy.
   _____

6 The marketing department will carry out extensive trials before launching the new product.
   _____

Past modals

Rewrite the sentences using the verbs in brackets.

1 She came at ten, but we open at nine o'clock.
   (should) _____

2 He's just arrived but we expected him ages ago.
   (should) _____

3 They launched the product but I'm not sure the market was ready for it.
   (might) _____

4 I went to Spain and regretted not going for longer.
   (could) _____

5 It was quite well-organised but we can make improvements.
   (could) _____

6 He isn't certain, but he thinks he made a mistake.
   (might) _____

Consolidation

Underline the correct forms of the words in *italics*.

The spirit of invention

No amount of failure can lessen the enthusiasm of the true inventor

MANY INNOVATIONS flop before they [1]*could get / get* onto the market. Some ideas [2]*should / could* never have been tried in the first place. But the inventive spirit refuses to give up. It's easy [3]*to forget / forgotten* that the history of invention is a huge collection of failed ideas. Tourism in space [4]*may still happen / may still have happened* some day but icebergs [5]*being towed / towing* to drought-stricken areas probably won't. One thing remains true though, trial and lots of error [6]*is embedded / embedded* in entrepreneurship. Ask every commuter trapped in traffic what is their dream and they will say, [7]*a flying car / it was a flying car.* Ford's prototype single-seat plane [8]*introduced / was introduced* in 1926. However, it [9]*was never produced / never went into production* by Ford. That didn't end the dream. Aviation enthusiast and Bureau of Air Commerce chief Eugene Vidal said government grants [10]*would be offered / were offered* to manufacturers of a 'poor man's airplane'. But still none were produced. A contemporary inventor Paul Moller recently explained that his skycar [11]*is / was* almost ready for launch and 'the automobile', he insists, [12]*'is / was* only an interim step on our evolutionary path to independence from gravity.' His invention [13]*was displayed / displayed* at a trade fair in Texas a few years ago. When commenting on the show he said that he had been happy with the initial interest people [14]*had shown / are showing.*

Vocabulary check

1 Complete the text with the correct option A–C.

Logistics on the move

A new breed of logistics operator takes advantage of new technology to create new markets

Logistics is a word most often seen on the side of trucks and is therefore mostly associated with the [1]_____ of goods from one place to another. But it has a bigger meaning, the management of the flow of material through an organisation from [2]_____ materials to finished goods. It might sound a simple enough business moving things around but it is growing more complex as new technology and greater use of the [3]_____ open new ways of passing around [4]_____ and selling products. This has opened up many new [5]_____ for the logistics industry.

E-commerce has encouraged a new generation of logistics [6]_____ to set up new companies. When you first [7]_____ a new e-business it is cheaper and more efficient to outsource the packing and delivery of products. It also reduces the initial investment and [8]_____ factor in setting up a new business.

Good logistics also play an important role in reducing the costly inventory problem of over [9]_____ and guaranteeing that there are no interruptions in the supply [10]_____.

1	A travel	B transport	C export
2	A raw	B basic	C component
3	A email	B software	C internet
4	A news	B stories	C information
5	A ways	B markets	C products
6	A entrepreneurs	B engineers	C businessmen
7	A begin	B launch	C commence
8	A inventory	B warehouse	C materials
9	A filling	B stocking	C supplying
10	A links	B flow	C chain

2 Complete the table below.

	verb	noun
1	innovate	
2		information
3	produce	
4		design
5	communicate	
6	invent	

Career skills

Summarising

Complete the dialogue with the phrases.

the important thing is   he reckons
she was going on and on about   he told me that
what she was trying to say was

A   It wasn't really clear but I think [1]_____ that we shouldn't over-use email.

B   Yeah, they're getting strict about personal emails, too. John met her yesterday and [2]_____ she was going to mention it at the meeting. [3]_____ they are going to check up on us.

A   I wouldn't mind but [4]_____ it as if it was the only information overload. I mean she sends about 20 emails a week to the whole staff.

B   Don't get upset. [5]_____ we have been given a warning in advance, that's all.

Dealing with questions

Match the answers to the questions.

1   Why did you leave your last job?
2   Why are your prices higher than the competitor's?
3   How do you deal with authority?
4   Can we have a market breakdown of that ten per cent rise?

a   Mutual respect is very important and I know my ideas will be listened to if I support them well.

b   As I had gone as far as I could in that area, I needed a new challenge.

c   Certainly, those figures will be available later, but they are not really what concern us here today.

d   We provide the highest quality and include a one-year guarantee and after-sales service in our price.

Reviewing achievement

Underline the incorrect extra word in each sentence.

1   There were just a couple of the things that I am a little concerned about.

2   Overall, I'd say for you and your team did quite a good job apart from being over budget.

3   We've had far too many problems areas with the quality of the software with the new application.

4   I think in future time you need to reduce the number of changes made before production.

5   That was great. I don't think the negotiation could have been gone any better. We're so pleased.

Pairwork

Unit 3 page 29 **Group B**

GEORGIO ARMANI Strategy presentation

1	Current sectors of activity:	scent watches furniture nightclubs	cosmetics fashion confectionery flowers	spectacles accessories cafés
2	Proposed new market:	Hotel industry		
3	Proposed project:	Joint venture with Emaar Properties to design ten new luxury hotels and four resorts		
4	Project duration:	8–10 years		
5	Strategic reasoning:	Competitors are already entering hotel market (Bulgari)		
6	Risks:	Travel and luxury industries follow same economic cycle Unstable market conditions Dilution of brand		
7	Advantages:	Generating positive publicity		

Unit 15 page 128 **Creativity quiz**

Scoring   Calculate your total score:

Never	score **one** point for each answer
Sometimes	score **three** points for each answer
Always	score **five** points for each answer

If you scored:

Between 0 and 9. You are the type of person who prefers to follow instructions and perform clearly defined tasks. To develop your creativity you need to adopt a more questioning approach to accepted ways of doing things and to put more trust in your imagination.

Between 10 and 15. You are able to find creative solutions to everyday problems and to produce new and interesting ideas. To do this more effectively you need to work on developing your skills in the areas where your scores were the lowest.

Between 16 and 20. You are a highly creative person who enjoys the challenge of resolving complex problems. You are able to analyse and synthesise existing information and to apply unconventional thinking to provide innovative solutions.
You could well be the next Jonathan Ive!

Unit 4   page 37 **Student A**

Answer your partner's questions about the following CEOs.

1 Bob Mendelsohn, former CEO of Royal & Sun Alliance, a large UK insurance company.

Severance deal:
- £2.4m
- £354,000 annual pension

Company performance:
- 90 per cent collapse in shares
- 12,000 job losses.

2 Sir Brian Moffat, former CEO of Corus, the Anglo-Dutch steelmaker.

Severance deal:
- A £300,000 a year pension.

Company performance:
- a £400m loss
- 99 per cent drop in share price
- 12,000 job losses.

Now ask Student B to give you the missing information about the following severance deals.

3 John Weston, former CEO of BAE Systems, the UK aerospace group.

Severance deal:

_____

_____

Company performance:

_____

_____

4 Sir Geoff Mulcahy, former CEO of Kingfisher, a UK retail giant.

Severance deal:

_____

_____

Company performance:

_____

Unit 5   page 48 **Group C – Amazon Watch**

You represent the native peoples of the Camisea region and the marine reserve at Paracas. The tribes have no desire to see their territory exploited within a market economy. The project presents many threats to local communities, such as:
- diseases brought in by outsiders are a health risk
- local fishing industry would be endangered by possible pollution
- social change with communities being replaced by outside workers
- long term disruption of the region by other new industries (logging and agriculture)
- erosion of the soil around the pipeline route and pollution of water source
- _____
- _____

Unit 11   page 100 **Dilemma Group B:** Watermark

The total budget that you have been given for the website is €10,000 for development and installation plus an annual maintenance budget of €1,000. You have also been told that it is essential that the site be up and running within five months – or earlier if possible. Your instructions concerning payment are to pay as little as possible up front and the remainder on delivery. You are aware that the estimate submitted by N-Vision is negotiable, within reason. But will you be able to obtain a quality site for less money than they are asking for? Look at N-Vision's estimate on page 141 and decide where you can negotiate discounts and where you will have to reduce the specification to make your target budget.

Unit 12   page 108 **Dilemma: Student B**

You are a resident of the town and oppose the sale of Hershey Foods. Use the following information to make your case.

- the town and the company are closely linked
- tourists visit the town because of the 'magic' created by its image of 'chocolate town'
- the buyer may cut jobs and this will be an economic disaster for the town
- Milton Hershey would never have sold (a 102-year-old former executive who knew him personally, said so and is involved in your lobby!)
- the interest generated by Hershey's $5.6bn gift is enough to finance a school
- many people in the trust are not from the town. They don't understand that the residents are protecting a 'way of life'

Unit 2   page 22 **Japanese culture**

The Japanese have a strong sense of belonging to 'the group'. In the context of work, the Japanese are loyal to their organisations and will usually accept management decisions which have been made to preserve or enhance the profitability of the organisation as a whole. Foreigners may have difficulty being accepted by the Japanese especially if they do not understand the subtleties of the Japanese language and the sometimes vague way that things are expressed. Negotiating and decision making often take place outside any formal meeting context and action is only taken after thorough consultation with the people concerned.

Unit 8   page 73 **Student A**

Look at the bar chart showing the European sales of the Italian food giant Parmalat, which went bankrupt in 2003 with debts of €14bn. Listen to your partner and complete the American sales for 1996–2003. Then describe the European sales to your partner.

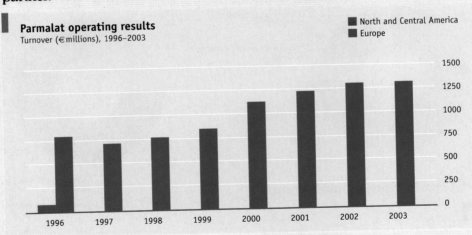

Parmalat operating results
Turnover (€millions), 1996–2003

Legend: ■ North and Central America ■ Europe

Ask Student A to give you the missing information about the following severance deals.

1 Bob Mendelsohn, former CEO of Royal & Sun Alliance, a large UK insurance company.

Severance deal:

_____

_____

Company performance:

_____

_____

2 Sir Brian Moffat, former CEO of Corus, the Anglo-Dutch steelmaker.

Severance deal:

_____

Company performance:

_____

_____

_____

Now answer your partner's questions about the following CEOs.

3 John Weston, former CEO of BAE Systems, the UK aerospace group.

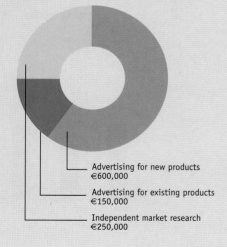

Severance deal:

- £1.5m pay off
- £3.7m pension fund

Company performance:

- falling profits
- shares were the lowest they'd been in 10 years.

4 Sir Geoff Mulcahy, former CEO of Kingfisher, a UK retail giant.

Severance deal:

- £502,000 in his last year with the company
- £1.4m pay off
- £790,000 a year pension despite:
- shares falling from 719p to 200p

---

1 **Human Resources costs**

External recruitment fees
€400,000

Performance-related bonuses
€400,000

Salaries
€3.2

2 **Production operating costs**

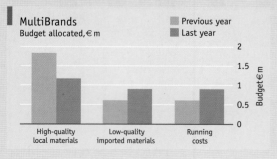

MultiBrands
Budget allocated, € m

■ Previous year
■ Last year

Budget €m

High-quality local materials / Low-quality imported materials / Running costs

3 **Sales and Marketing costs**

Advertising for new products
€600,000

Advertising for existing products
€150,000

Independent market research
€250,000

Estimate

NVISION

1.	**Price per page**	• (Standard graphics)	€100
		• (High-quality graphics)	€150
		Total 8 x 150 =	**€1,200**

2. Interactive features

Allowing interaction with customers and the creation of an online community.

	• Forum	€300
	• News	€300
	• Chat	€300
	Total =	**€900**

3. Customer payment system

	• Manual (all transactions managed by Watermark after email order confirmation)	€300
	• Fully automated (secured, automated online invoicing and payment system)	€2,500
	Total =	**€2,500**

4. Hosting (hardware systems for the site located at N-Vision's office)

	• Shared server (payable every month)	€100*
	• Client owned server	€3,500
	Total =	**€3,500**

5. Content Modification (N-Vision 'Content Master' software allows clients to easily update the content of their own site)

	• Content Master software	€4,000
	• Training	€1,000
	Total =	**€5,000**

Total investment for site design and hardware	€13,100

6. Helpline (telephone and email) and maintenance charges per month €100

Total maintenance costs €100 per month

This would mean Watermark would be renting server space on an N-Vision shared server for €100 a month rather than buying their own exclusive server, which N-Vision is offering at €3,500

Transco, a UK pipeline company, which was originally part of British Gas opted for the Safety Charity Challenge when many other attempts to introduce a safety culture had failed the company. It dramatically reduced accidents (33 per cent in 18 months) saving 2,521 workdays! It also led to huge cost savings and generated a lot of good publicity, which had a positive effect on workforce morale. Efficiency also improved greatly. The challenge was also very beneficial for the charity Mencap, which deals with people with learning disabilities.

The Institute for Business Ethics says, 'If a way can be found to improve both the productivity of the company and the well-being of the community, then necessity will become a virtue.'

Unit 11   page 100 **Dilemma Group A: N-Vision**

N-Vision is a young company and it needs to obtain new contracts to finance its continued expansion. Experience has shown that new clients represent a long-term investment for the company as they very often request additional work to upgrade their sites once they are up and running. It is therefore very important for you to conclude a deal with Watermark. The suggestions that you have made in your estimate are based on N-Vision's experience of website design and that is why you have sometimes included top range features. The arguments you will use for each of the components of the proposal are the following:

Graphics – high-quality graphics are essential to attract customers.

Interactive modules – their usefulness depends on how interactive the customer wishes the site to be.

Customer payment – a fully automated system is complicated and will take longer to build.

Hosting – it is best for you to have a client owned server which you arrange to purchase. A site hosted on a shared server is exposed to security and traffic problems that may originate from the other sites that share the same server.

Content modification – this is very important as it gives the customer greater freedom and also makes them dependent on N-vision software.

Helpline – essential for all customers.

You are prepared to offer a maximum total discount of ten per cent on your proposal, on condition that the customer pays 50 per cent of the total cost upfront with delivery in six to eight months. Any modification of delivery dates and payment will reduce the discount that you can give. Conduct the negotiation with the Watermark representatives.

Unit 12   page 108 **Dilemma: Student A**

You are a member of the board of trustees that wishes to sell Hershey Foods. Use the following information to make your case.

- it is too risky to have only one source of investment
- we make good financial decisions and will invest the money from the sale well
- the trust needs the money to expand the school from 1,200 to 1,500 students
- the company does not play the same role as 40 years ago
- many employees do not live in the town anymore
- most residents work for Hershey Medical Center and Hershey Entertainment which manages the town's $200 million tourism industry – not the chocolate company
- Hershey town needs to move with the times and not live in the past

Unit 5   page 48 **Group B – Peruvian government representatives**

You are representatives of the Peruvian government. Camisea is a critical element for the economic development of your country for the following reasons:

- cheaper electricity supply for the country
- improved standard of living (+ one per cent for GDP)
- increase in foreign investment in Peru
- creation of up to 6,000 jobs during construction phase
- tax income (over $100m per year for Cuzco region and $100m for the government)
- _____
- _____

You are the CEO of the Renault group and the partnership with Nissan was largely your idea as you considered it to be a key element of your strategy to make Renault a truly international company. If the alliance fails, it will be disaster for the company. Your career is now coming to an end and you plan to hand over control of the group within the next five years. Anyone who can turn Nissan back to profit within a relatively short time might be just the right person to take your place. Carlos Ghosn might just be that person. You know that he has a reputation as a man of action who takes quick decisions and who likes to do things his own way. Make a list of the arguments that you will use to persuade him to accept the position.

- If he is successful, he could become the next director of the group.

- _____

- _____

Harley Davidson
Proposals for Strategic Leadership Council meeting.

Product development approach

- Invest in new lighter and faster Harley Davidson models. This might attract a younger purchaser and would change the image of HD products, which are associated with heavier cruising bikes.

Acquisition approach

- Harley Davidson has acquired Buell, a small manufacturer of sports motorcycles. This could be an opportunity to introduce a new range of sports bikes that would be marketed by existing HD dealers but sold under the Buell brand.

- Aggressive foreign expansion. HD has poor market penetration in Europe and the Far East. Huge potential markets exist, especially in China which has annual sales of 14 million motorcycles.

Marketing approach

- Concentrate on developing the merchandising sources of income by signing deals to develop the HD brand on clothing and fashion accessories.

Distribution approach

- Review the HD dealer network. At the moment the dealers are independent operations which place orders with the parent company. It might be possible to develop sales through other outlets (buyers clubs, specialist stores).

- Develop a strong internet presence, possibly with direct internet sales.

eBay has a strict company policy concerning exactly what items can be listed for sale on its site. see http://pages.ebay.com/help/policies/hub.html for more information

1 Sold at a 'charity auction' by the Tiger Woods foundation for $425,000
2 The former Atlas missile silo was bought for $2.1 million.
3 Withdrawn from sale (bids were rumoured to have reached 10 million)
4 $47,000 for a fifteen minute appearance on the 'Politically Incorrect' show
5 $35 for one square meter of the isle of Clett
6 Withdrawn from sale

The price of Prosperity

Local factory Jackson & Sons are in court this week on charges of polluting local rivers and lakes with chemicals from their profitable new factory extension.

CITY DEVELOPERS
PUT PEOPLE ON THE STREET

LAMBERT ASSOCIATES, London's biggest inner city property developer, makes hundreds homeless to create more luxury office space.

Poisoning the Public

Consumer Action group demands recall of Farma's sleeping pills after traces of poison were found in some batches.

Greed before People

Hundreds of job losses as clothing manufacturer Nice Fit Ltd. moves production to South East Asia.

Shareholders in arms!

JEFFERSONS, the major arms maker, faces a shareholder revolt at an urgent meeting today after laying off hundreds of local employees shortly before announcing a $4m performance-related bonus for CEO Alan Carmichaels.

You represent the consortium of companies involved in the construction and management of the Camisea project. For you the project could lead to large profits. However, you will have to find advantages of the project that will benefit the region and its people, such as:

- creation of jobs
- subcontracting opportunities for local Peruvian companies
- transfer of technology and know-how to Peru
- improved standard of living for the local people
- prospects of further economic development
- _____
- _____

You are the manager of Renault's engineering division where you have worked for the last three years following an international career in the USA and Latin America with the Michelin tyre company. You know that Louis Schweitzer is considering you for the position of CEO at Nissan but you have certain reservations about accepting the assignment:

- you have no experience of working with the Japanese
- is your direct style of management compatible with the Japanese style of doing business?
- you would need to cut costs by eliminating jobs and factories – would this be politically acceptable to the Japanese employees and authorities?
- failure in this mission could damage your long-term career prospects

How will you respond if Mr Schweitzer offers you the position? Make a list of the things that you would like Mr Schweitzer to do if you are to accept the position.

Volkswagen AG

Summary of main problems:

▶ collapse of Latin American market – VW had invested heavily in Brazil
▶ poor performance of new models (low sales of luxury cars and new Golf)
▶ fall in dollar revenues from US operations
▶ increased competition in Asian markets (reduced market share in China from 50 per cent to 30 per cent)
▶ shrinking European market for medium-sized cars
▶ cheaper company brands (Seat/Skoda) are affecting margins and profitability

Achtung!
Volkswagen share price €

1 ZephGen Wind Power

Wind power is one of the world's untapped power sources. Our modular platforms are designed to be used offshore in locations where natural wind sources are abundant. Using improved technology, they can provide an invaluable alternative energy source and an investment opportunity for both private sector and public investors.

2 Rainbow Systems Packaging

We have developed special thermal additives that change colour when exposed to extreme temperatures and ultra-violet rays. Potential applications include packaging materials that will automatically reveal exposure to heat or UV rays.

3 Open Tour Mobile Guides

Open Tour will allow customers all over the world to receive audio guided tours for all the principal tourist destinations via their mobile phones. An easily accessible and affordable alternative to carrying guidebooks.

4 VoxData Mood Recognition Software

Our revolutionary voice recognition software makes it possible to monitor the dynamics of customer calls. Detecting variations in voice patterns that reveal emotional intensity, VoxData can be used to monitor call centre operations and to provide detailed statistics to help managers improve performance.

Unit 10   page 92 **Decision**

Hello! magazine was ordered by London's High Court to pay £1,033,156 to *OK!*. The judge also ruled that *Hello!* had breached the couple's commercial confidentiality but rejected their claim that the photos intruded on their privacy. *Hello!* was told to pay the couple $14,600 in total, including only $3,750 each for the 'emotional hurt' caused. After a second hearing, it was decided that *Hello!* pay 75 per cent of the legal costs for the first court case and 85 per cent of the costs of the hearing which decided who should pay the legal costs!

Unit 12   page 108 **Decision**

Extract from *The Economist* 'Bitter-Sweet' 21 September 2002

ON 17 SEPTEMBER 2002 the board announced the abandonment of its plans to sell its controlling stake in Hershey Foods. It was seen as an important success for lobbies and protest groups everywhere. On the other hand, *The Economist* magazine business expert believes that in the long run the town may live to regret its apparent victory:

"The ultimate loser may be Hershey Foods. Although its new management is doing well, the firm is again protected from the risk of unwanted takeover, with all that can mean for dampening incentives and innovation. There may well be missed opportunities – a multinational owner like Nestlé could have taken Hershey's cheap chocolate into big new markets such as China. Hershey itself has never been able to persuade anyone but Americans to eat Hershey Kisses. So there may eventually be reason for the townsfolk of Hershey to regret this week's events. But for now their victory must taste exceedingly sweet" ■

Unit 13   page 118 **Decision**

Lambert Associates, a company that has done much to improve the architecture and the working conditions of thousands of office workers in central London, is once again planning to transform a building, which badly needs a facelift, into luxury offices.

The company is aware that the occupants are worried about their future and deeply regrets not informing them sooner about the budget that has been set aside to ensure that they won't find themselves in the street. Not only does each resident have six months rent-free to find new housing but Lambert Associates intends to give them a six-month extension if they need it. In addition, they are helping the residents to find new housing in residential areas of the city and will pay their moving costs. 'We have always put people before profit and this situation is no exception,' said the communication manager at the company. 'We are confident that we can find a win-win situation for everyone.'

Unit 14   page 126 **Decision**

The Tesco case study: Trouser suit

Nov 22nd 2001 | NEW YORK

The European Court sides with Levi Strauss in its battle with Tesco.

On November 20th the European Court of Justice decided that Tesco, a UK supermarket chain, should not be allowed to import jeans made by America's Levi Strauss from outside the European Union and sell them at cut-rate prices without getting permission first from the jeans maker. Ironically, the ruling is based on an EU trademark directive that was designed to protect local, not US, manufacturers from price dumping. The idea is that any brand-owning firm should be allowed to position its goods and segment its markets as it sees fit: Levi's jeans, just like Gucci handbags, must be allowed to be expensive.

Glossary

asset *n* [C] something belonging to an individual or business that has value or the power to earn money: *The company has recently sold some of its assets to an Australian investor.* Collocations *tangible assets, intangible assets, fixed assets, liquid assets*

company *n* [C] a legally registered business. There are many different types of companies: holding company (holds the share capital of one or more other companies) joint stock company (registered company or limited company) public limited or listed company (company whose shares are traded on the stock exchange) subsidiary (company owned by a parent company) Synonyms corporation *n* [C] AmE concern *n* [C] business *n* [C]

competition *n* [U] rivalry between businesses that are operating in the same market: *The competition is getting tougher every year.* – compete *v* [I] – competitor *n* [C] – competitive *adj* – competitiveness *n* [U] Collocations *competitive advantage*

entrepreneur *n* [C] someone who starts a company, arranges business deals and takes risks: *Entrepreneurs have always played a key role in the economy.* – entrepreneurial *adj* – entrepreneurship *n* [U]

freelance *n* [C] someone who works for different companies and is not employed by one. Freelancers usually receive fixed payments and not a salary: *We're going to use a freelance designer for the company website.* – freelancer *n* [C] – freelance *adj*

hierarchy *n* [C] system of authority within an organisation: *Many Swedish firms have very flat hierarchies.* – hierarchical *adj* Collocations *flat hierarchy, steep hierarchy, traditional hierarchy*

merger *n* [C] the creation of a new company by joining two separate companies: *The merger will have to be approved by the authorities.* – merge *v* [I,T]

share *n* [C] a unit of the capital of a company. Shares in listed companies can be bought and sold on the stock market: *Investors are having to pay a higher price for the company's shares.* – shareholder *n* [C] stockholder *n* [C] US – shareholding *n* [C] Synonym stock *n* [C] AmE Collocations *share capital, share certificate, share dealing, share issue, share price*

trade union *n* [C] an organisation that exists to protect the rights of employees in a company: *The trade union is in pay negotiations with the employer.* Synonym labor union *n* [C] AmE

appraise *v* (T) to assesss the value of something. Staff are regularly appraised to see if they have met the objectives that they are given: *The department manager will appraise each employee individually.* – appraisal *n* [C] – appraisee *n* [C] – appraisor *n* [C] Collocations *annual appraisal, performance appraisal*

authority 1 *n* [U] the power to impose decisions: *The managers in our company have a great deal of authority.* – authorise *v* (T) – authorisation *n* [U] – authoritative *adj* – authoritarian *adj* Collocations *lines of authority* **2** *n* [C] a public institution which is in charge of enforcing regulations or administering a government service: *The public health authority.*

autonomy *n* [U] the freedom to make your own decisions without having to request authorisation: *I've always believed that it's best to give staff as much autonomy as possible.* – autonomous *adj*

coach 1 *n* [C] person who is responsible for training a team or an individual: *He's a very successful football coach.* **2** *v* [T] to train people to help them to acquire particular skills: *I'm responsible for coaching two new people in the department.*

delegate *v* [T] to give responsibility to someone at a lower level in the hierarchy to enable them to take decisions: *Managers need to delegate more routine tasks to junior members of staff.* – delegation *n* [U]

motivate *v* [T] make someone willing to work harder: *He's very good at motivating his sales team.* – motivation *n* [U] – motivational *adj* – motivated *adj* Synonym encourage *v* [T] Collocations *highly-motivated, motivational skills, motivation techniques*

objective *n* [C] a goal that has been fixed for people to achieve: *I have a meeting with my line manager to fix my objectives every six months.* Synonyms goal *n* [C] aim *n* [C] target *n* [C] Collocations *set / fix / establish / achieve / meet objectives*

staff 1 *n* [plural] the employees of an organisation: *The new manager will be joining the staff in November.* **2** *v* [I] to provide workers for an organisation: *Each of our centres is staffed by expert personnel.* Synonyms personnel *n* [U] employees *n* [C] workers *n* [C] Collocations *staff morale, staff turnover*

subordinate *n* [C] a person who works under a more senior member of staff: *I have six subordinates that report to me.* – subordinate *v* [T]

supervise v [T] to control the work of other people in order to make sure that it is properly done: *We need to supervise the trainees very closely.* – supervision n [U] – supervisory adj Synonym manage v [T]

task n [C] a piece of work that has to be done. *Tasks are generally assigned to employees at the start of the week.* Synonym duty n [C] Collocations *assign / delegate a task, task-based, task-driven, task force*

Unit 3 Strategy

analysis n [C] the work of studying data and information: *Detailed analysis of our results shows that productivity has increased only marginally.* – analyse v [T] – analyst n [C] Collocations *financial analysis*

campaign n [C] a planned operation which aims to achieve a particular result: *A new campaign by activists has forced the company to reconsider some of its policies.* – campaign v [I] [+ for/against] – campaigner n [C] Collocations *advertising campaign, marketing campaign, political campaign*

growth n [U] an increase in the size or quantity of something: *Research suggests that there will be significant growth in the market for women's products.* – grow v [I] Collocations *growth rate*

industry n [C] the production of goods using capital and labour: *The automobile industry is facing increased competition.* – industrial adj – industrialise v [T] – industrialisation n [C] Collocations *manufacturing industry, service industry, industrial relations*

market share n [U] the proportion of the total market that is supplied by a particular company: *Our objective is to increase our European market share by five per cent this year.* – market-sharing n [U] Collocations *increase / lose / take / win market share*

opportunity n [C] a situation with future potential: *Japan represents a great opportunity for our new brand.* Collocations *lose / sieze / take an opportunity*

resources n [C] this includes the capital, personnel and knowledge that an organisation has at its disposal: *A key element of the new strategy is the more effective use of our resources.* Collocations *human resources, financial resources*

sales 1 n [plural] the value of the goods and services sold during a period: *The company reported sales of $42 million during the first quarter.* **2** the department responsible for the activity of selling goods and services to customers: *I'll put you through to our sales department.* – salesman/woman n [C] –

salesclerk n [C] AmE Collocations *sales agent, sales call, sales conference, sales department, sales drive, sales figures, sales forecast, sales manager, sales outlet, sales pitch, sales promotion, sales representative, sales talk*

strategy n [C] a plan of action to enable a firm to compete: *As part of our new strategy we are developing closer links with our suppliers.* – strategic adj – strategically adv Collocations *develop / revise a strategy, strategic alliance, strategic management, strategic planning, strategic business unit (SBU)*

supply n [U] the amount of goods or services available on a market at a certain time: *Improved production techniques will increase the supply of raw materials.* – supply v [T] – supplier n [C] – supplies n [C] Collocations *order supplies, supply and demand, supply chain management, supply side, oversupply*

threat n [C] a potential danger to the interests of a company: *Deregulation of the market is a real threat to established telecom operators.* – threaten v [T] – threatening adj – threateningly adv

Unit 4 Pay

board n [C] the group of directors elected by the shareholders to manage a company: *The board has approved the director's salary.* Collocations *board of directors, board meeting, boardroom*

budget n [C] an account of probable future income and expenditure during a fixed period: *We are currently preparing the budget for next year.* – budget v [I] – budgetary adj Collocations *be on / over / under budget, budget deficit, budget surplus, meet a budget*

compensation n [U] payment, including salary and other incentives like stock options: *The best paid executives received more than $10 million in compensation last year.* – compensate v [T] Collocations *compensation deal, compensation package*

contract n [C] a document setting out an agreement between two or more parties: *Under the new contract the company becomes the exclusive distributor for North America.* – contractor n [C] – sub-contractor n [C] Collocations *agree a contract, be under contract, breach a contract, negotiate a contract, review a contract, sign a contract, terminate a contract*

damages n [plural] an amount of money paid to a person who has suffered an injustice: *The company paid damages to staff who were unfairly dismissed.*

legal action n [C,U] using the law to defend one's rights: *The consumer association said it will consider legal action.* Synonyms litigation n [U]

148 ■ Glossary

law suit *n* [C] Collocations *take legal action, win a legal action*

pay 1 *n* [U] money earned by an employee as a salary or wage: *Some employees are complaining that their pay has not increased in line with inflation.* – payment *n* [C] Collocations *pay as you earn (PAYE), pay freeze, pay rise, payroll, pay-slip, pay talks* **2** to give money to someone in exchange for items or services: *We're paying more than the market rate.*

pension *n* [C] a regular payment made to a person after they have retired from active work: *Some businesses have decided to ask their staff to contribute another one per cent towards their pensions.* Collocations *pension fund, pension contribution*

reward *v* [T] to give a payment for services performed or for excellent work or behaviour: *We like to reward our staff when they reach the objectives.* – reward *n* [C,U] – rewarding *adj*

salary *n* [C,U] an amount of money paid every month to an employee in exchange for their services: *Salaries are always paid in the local currency.* – salaried *adj* Collocations *be on a salary of, earn a salary, negotiate a salary, salary scale*

severance deal / pay *n* [C,U] money paid by an employer when an employee's services are terminated: *Severance pay for top executives has increased significantly in recent years.*

stock option *n* [C] an option given to executive employees allowing them to buy shares in the company at a favourable price: *Microsoft has announced that it plans to end stock options for employees.*

Unit 5 Development

consortium *n* [C] an association between two or more companies to work together on a specific project (usually a major construction or engineering project): *SK Gas has formed a consortium with automakers to produce gas-powered vehicles.*

cost 1 *n* [C] the price paid for something: *The total cost for the new equipment will be $50,000.* **2** the money that is required to produce or sell something: *It looks like production and labour costs will be higher than we expected.* – cost *v* [I] Synonym overheads *n* [C] Collocations *fixed costs, variable costs, cost-cutting, cost control, cost-effective, occur a cost*

development 1 *n* [C] the growth and expansion of a business, industry or economy: *The OECD provides advice and assistance on all aspects of development.* **2** research to produce new, improved products: *Our company is actively pursuing the development of new biotechnology solutions.* **3** a change or alteration: *Another recent development has been the arrival of Asian companies on the market.* – developer *n* [C] – developing *adj* Collocations *research and development (R&D), developing countries*

loan *n* [C] money lent to an individual or organisation: *The World Bank has agreed to a five-year loan of $125m.* – loan *v* [T] Collocations *apply for a loan, bank loan, interest on a loan, take out a loan*

negotiation *n* [C] the process of negotiating a business deal: *The success of the negotiations will depend on the financial terms of the deal.* – negotiate *v* [I,T] – negotiator *n* [C] Synonyms *talks n [plural]* Collocations *negotiate an agreement / a deal, negotiation skills*

prosperity *n* [U] a state of being rich, having economic success: *The nation's future prosperity will depend on developing a highly-skilled workforce.* – prosper *v* [I] – prosperous *adj*

reserve 1 *n* [C] the amount of something kept for future use: *Shell has revised its estimate of available oil reserves.* **2** an amount of money set aside from profits: *Ten per cent of earnings have been transferred to reserves.* – reserve *v* [T] Synonym resources *n* [U] Collocations *hold in reserve, use up reserves*

revenue *n* [C] money received especially from selling goods and services: *Revenues have increased by six per cent to £183m.*

wealth *n* [U] the amount of money or possessions owned by an individual, organisation or country: *Accumulating wealth is the key to financial independence.* – wealthy *adj* Collocations *acquire / accumulate wealth*

Unit 6 Marketing

barrier to entry *n* [C] any factor which prevents new competition from entering a market: *A strong brand can become a barrier to entry in some markets, while a simple product cannot.*

benefit *n* [C] an advantage or an improvement: *One benefit of the new design is that it can be installed easily.* – benefit [+ from] *v* – beneficial *adj*

brand *n* [C] the identity of a product or service: *Eastman Kodak is a premier brand in traditional and digital imaging.* – brand *v* [T] Collocations *brand image, brand leader, brand loyalty, brand* manager, brand management, brand name, brand-stretching, cross-branding, own brand, premium brand

consumer n [C] a person who buys products and/or services: *Nokia is committed to providing consumers with the information they need.* – consume v [T] – consumption n [U] Collocations *consumer goods, consumer research, consumer survey*

logo n [C] a sign or symbol used as a trademark to represent a company or a brand: *The Nike 'swoosh' is an instantly recognisable logo.*

marketing mix n [U] the four different components of marketing: **1 place** n [C] the distribution and delivery of goods to market **2 price** n [C] the amount of money for which something can be sold. – price v [T] Collocations *cost price, cut price, fixed price, list price, retail price , purchase price, recommended price, wholesale price, price-list, price-tag, price war* **3 product** n [C] normally a manufactured item but also refers to everything that surrounds the product: the brand, the packaging, the product's features and performance characteristics. **4 promotion** n [C] activities that help sell a product

premium n [C] a price that is higher than the standard price, usually due to higher quality: *Organically grown foods are sold at a premium.* Collocations *premium rate*

promotion n [C] a method of communicating and publicising a product: *America Online plans to launch a promotion on Thursday that will let its members download full-feature films.* – promote v [T] – promotional adj Collocations *seasonal promotion, promotional campaign, promotional price*

point of sale abbreviation **POS** n [C] the place where a consumer can buy a product or service: *New electronic systems can approve credit for customers at the point of sale.*

Unit 7   Outsourcing

back office n [C] the departments of a financial company where routine admistrative tasks are done without direct contact with customers: *Efficient management of the back office can reduce costs.*

business process n [C] any activity that is essential for a firm to conduct its business: *Organisations that have complete control over their business processes are the most productive.* Collocations *business process re-engineering*

database n [C] an organised set of information stored in a computer: *We're currently updating all our customer files in the database.*

downsize v [I] to reduce the number of employees in an organisation: *European companies are continuing to downsize their manufacturing operations.* – downsize v [T] Synonyms lay off v [T]

knowledge work n [U] work that involves developing or using knowledge: *The profitability of most business today depends more on knowledge work than on manual work.* – knowledge worker n [C]

offshoring n [U] transferring work to an outside supplier based in another country: *Offshoring is only suitable for tasks that have been clearly defined and can be managed at a distance.* – offshore adj – offshore n [U] Synonyms outsource v [T]

outsource v [T] transferring work to an outside supplier: *We are planning to outsource all of our IT operations to an Indian supplier.* – outsourcing n [U] Synonyms subcontract v [T]

overhead n [C] a cost that does not vary with output (e.g. rent, salaries): *The pressure on corporate mangement to reduce overheads is increasing.* Synonyms fixed cost n [C]

pilot project n [C] a trial project to test performance: *The pilot project will start operating in June.*

productivity n [U] The relationship between the output of goods and the resources needed to produce them: *Productivity has continued to grow strongly.*

saving n [C] money and materials saved by economical working: *New construction techniques resulted in a saving of 25 per cent of operation and maintenance costs.* – savings [plural] Synonym economy n [U] Collocations *cost saving, make savings*

service provider n [C] a company that provides services for users especially in computer networks: *There are several issues to consider when selecting a service provider.*

shortage n [C] a lack or scarcity of something: *Silicon Valley is facing a shortage of skilled programmers.*

Unit 8   Finance

balance sheet n [C] a statement showing the wealth of a business or organisation at a particular date. The balance sheet has two parts showing assets and liabilities: *Buildings and machinery are assets that should be listed on the balance sheet.* Synonyms statement of financial position *n* [C] *AmE*

bankrupt *adj* unable to pay your debts: *The company is almost bankrupt and will need to secure a loan to survive.* – bankrupt *v, n* [C] – bankruptcy *n* [U] Synonyms insolvent *adj AmE*

bottom line *n* [C] the last line on a financial document which shows the final result (total profit once all costs have been deducted): *Falling sales are going to have a negative impact on the bottom line.*

expense 1 *n* [C] money spent: *We have significantly reduced our expenses over the last five years.* – expenditure *n* [C] Synonyms spending *n* [U] **2** *n* [C] money spent by an employee that can be claimed back: *I put the restaurant bill on expenses.* Collocations *expense account, expenses claim form, claim expenses*

financial statement *n* [C] a document showing the state of the finances of an organisation or business: *Financial statements must be completed by the end of August.*

forecast *n* [C] an estimate of a future situation: *According to forecasts, prices will rise more slowly next year.* – forecast *v* [T] Synonyms projection *n* [C]

income statement *n* [C] *AmE* a financial statement showing revenue, expenditure and profit from operations during a given period: *Enron's income statement did not accurately reflect its losses.* Synonyms profit and loss account *n* [C] *BrE* statement of earnings *n* [C] *AmE*

mismanagement *n* [U] poor quality management: *Lack of cashflow is often due to mismanagement.* – mismanage *v* [T]

profit and loss account *n* [C] *BrE* a financial statement showing revenue, expenditure and profit from operations during a given period: *Ahold's profit and loss account did not show all its losses.* Synonyms income statement *n* [C] *AmE* statement of earnings *n* [C] *AmE*

regulator *n* [C] a government agency responsible for overseeing a profession or an activity: *Stock market regulators are in charge of protecting investors.* – regulation *n* [C] Synonyms controller *n* [C]

Securities Exchange Commission abbreviation **SEC** *n* the US agency responsible for stock market regulation: *The SEC is currently investigating ten cases of fraud.*

accountable *adj* responsible for the effects of your actions: *Managers are accountable for the performance of their employees.* Synonyms responsibile [+ for] *adj*

applicant *n* [C] a person who is applying for a position: *All applicants are asked to provide a letter of reference.* – apply [+ for] *v* [I] – application *n* [C] Synonyms candidate *n* [C]

assign *v* [T] give someone a particular task to do: *Employees are assigned duties that correspond to their skills and training.* – assignment *n* [C]

cover letter *n* [C] a letter written to an employer in response to a job advertisement: *Candidates should send a cover letter with a copy of their CV.*

curriculum vitae abbreviation **CV** *n* [C] a document that gives details of a person's experience and qualifications: *Her CV is fairly typical for a business graduate.* Synonyms resumé *n* [C] *AmE*

deadline *n* [C] the date by which something has to be completed: *The deadline for applications has been extended until the 25 May.* Collocations *fix a deadline, meet a deadline, miss a deadline, set a deadline*

empower *v* [T] give someone the power or ability to do something: *Staff are empowered to shape their career development.* – empowerment *n* [U]

hire *v* [T] employ someone: *Businesses are hiring as job growth booms.* – hire *n* [C] Synonyms recruit *v* [T] employ *v* [T] Collocations *hiring and firing, hiring manager*

payroll *n* [U] **1** a list of the employees in an organisation **2** the administration of employee pay: *Salaries are calculated according to the number of days that employees are on the payroll.* Collocations *payroll management, cut/reduce the payroll*

qualification *n* [C] an examination passed at school or university: *Candidates must have qualifications in accounting.* – qualify *v* [I] – qualified *adj*

resumé *n* [C] *AmE* a document that gives details of a candidate's experience and qualifications: *Preparing a good resumé should be the starting point for all job seekers.* Synonyms Curriculum Vitae *BrE*

screen v [T] to examine or test people: *Each candidate is screened for education, experience, expertise and salary.*

train v [T] to teach someone the skills of a particular job or activity: *Staff are trained to watch for situations where they may be required to help.* – training n [U] – trainee n [C] – trainer n [C]

Unit 10   Counterfeiting

copycat n [C] the term for someone who copies the work of another person: *The Australian government has announced that it is cracking down on copycats.*

copyright n [U] the legal right that belongs to the person who has created a new artistic work or piece of software: *All of the graphics and editorial content on this site are protected under US copyright.*

currency n [C] the type of money that is used by a particular country or trading bloc: *The euro is the currency of most member states of the European Union.* Synonyms money n [U] Collocations *foreign currency, hard currency, currency dealer, currency exchange rate, currency trading*

defraud v [T] to cheat another person by taking something that they own: *He admitted defrauding his employer of more than £2m.*

enforce v [T] to make people obey a law or rule: *Enforcing a patent can be a long and expensive process.* – enforcement n [U] – enforceable adj

fake n [C] a copy or imitation of a genuine article: *Experts have identified the components as fakes.* – fake v [T] Synonyms copy v [C] – copy n [C]

file-swapping n [U] exchanging files between computers on a network: *Record companies tried to close down the illegal file-swapping website.*

infringement n [U] a breach of the law or of another person's rights: *The company is being sued over infringements of copyright technology.*

intellectual property n [U] something that a person or business has invented and which is protected by patent: *All international businesses are having to spend more on protecting their intellectual property.*

patent n [C] a special right given to the inventor of a machine or process: *Some governments do not recognise patents on software.* – patent v [T] – patented adj Synonyms copyright n [C,U] Collocations *patent pending, patent office*

piracy n [U] infringement of copyrights: *The association has launched a campaign to fight software piracy.*

profitability n [U] the ability of a business to earn profits: *Increased labour costs have reduced our profitability.* – profit n [C] – profit v [I] – profitable adj

trademark n [C] a special, registered picture or symbol that is associated with a particular brand or product: *Our trademark is now well-known in most countries in the region.*

Unit 11   Markets

bid n [C] an offer to buy something at a stated price: *All bids must be submitted in writing.* – bid v [I,T] – bidder n [C] – bidding n [U] Synonyms offer n [C] Collocations *make/accept/reject a bid, takeover bid*

business to business abbreviation **B2B** adj refers to any business or correspondence between two companies: *The B2B sector will be the biggest growth area in internet traffic.*

dealer n [C] a person who specialises in trading a particular type of goods: *The company only uses authorised dealers who are fully trained.* – deal n [C] – deal v [I,T] Collocations *foreign exchange dealer, broker-dealer, dealership, make/reach/conclude a deal, raw deal*

demand n [C,U] the quantity required to supply orders: *Total petroleum demand has increased by one per cent.* Collocations *supply and demand*

e-business n [U] business to business relationships conducted using internet technology: *IBM is one of the leading suppliers of e-business solutions.*

e-commerce n [U] selling activities that are conducted using internet technology: *Some consumers still lack confidence in e-commerce.*

glitch n [C] a minor fault with a computer program or machine: *A glitch in the computer system has led to the cancellation of several flights.* Synonyms malfunction n [C] bug n [C]

gross v [T] to calculate revenue before tax and other charges have been deducted: *The film grossed $8.5m in the first two weeks.* – gross adj Collocations *gross profit, gross margins, gross national product, gross domestic product (GDP)*

inventory n [C] a list of the stocks held by a business: *New software has made it possible to control inventory more accurately.* Synonyms stock n [C]

market research n [U] the work of finding out what kind of goods consumers want: *Conducting online surveys is a new and promising approach to market research.*

mass market *n* [U] the market for standardised consumer products: *Licensing is one way for small businesses to enter the mass market.* – mass-market *adj*

merchandising *n* [U] toys, clothes and other products based on a popular film, TV show, etc and sold to make additional profits: *Star Wars merchandising made far more profit than the films.*

price setting *n* [U] fixing the prices at which goods and services will be sold: *In price setting you try to estimate how much customers will be prepared for an item*

real estate *n* [U] property in the form of land or houses: *Investing in real estate is not as risk free as some people think.* Synonyms property *n* [U] *BrE* realty *n* [U] *AmE* Collocations estate agent *BrE*

tender *n* [C] a written offer by a supplier to provide goods or services at a certain price: *Your tender has been accepted at the agreed price.* – tender *v* [I,T]

Unit 12 Lobbies

aid *n* [U] assistance given to a country or organisation in difficulty: *The World Bank is repeating its call for rich countries to increase the amount of aid given to the poorest nations.* – aid *v* [T]

boycott *n* [C] a protest where people refuse to buy or use a product or service: *The consumer group is calling for the boycott of all tobacco products.* – boycott *v* [T]

charity *n* [C] a non profit-making organisation that collects goods and money in order to provide assistance: *The charity managed to raise £3m for homeless people in the UK.*

debt relief *n* [U] the cancellation or reduction of a debt: *The government is firmly committed to a programme of debt relief.*

demonstration *n* [C] a march to publicly protest about something: *The demonstration will take place at G7 summit on 10 June.*

fair trade *n* [U] a movement which promotes fairer trading conditions for developing countries: *Fair trade gives consumers an opportunity to help change the world.*

grant *n* [C] a sum of money given to a person or organisation to help them to pay for something: *The Central Development Fund has awarded a grant of $7.5m.* – grant *v* [T]

income *n* [C,U] money received by a person, family or organisation: *In some parts of the country incomes have fallen by as much as 25 per cent.* Synonyms revenue *n* [C] Collocations income tax, gross income, net income

litigation *n* [U] legal action against an individual or organisation: *Litigation has increased significantly over the years.* – litigate *v* [U] – litigator *n* [C]

lobby *v* [T] to try to persuade a government or organisation to change a policy or situation: *Big companies are lobbying the president to open up marine reserves for oil drilling.* – lobby *n* [U] lobbyist *n* [U]

petition *n* [C] a document signed by many people asking someone in authority to change something: *So far, five thousand people have signed the petition.* – petition [+ against/for] *v* [I,T]

pressure group *n* [C] a group that tries to influence the opinions of other people: *The pressure group is cordinating the protests.*

protectionism *n* [U] protecting a country's trade by taxing foreign goods: *Protectionism usually increases the prices of basic goods to the consumer.*

quota *n* [C] an official limit on the amount of something: *Quotas have been imposed on 25 categories of imported clothing.*

subsidy *n* [C] money given by a government to certain producers to help them to produce without losing money: *World Bank economists are urging rich countries to cut subsidies to certain industries.* – subsidise *v* [T]

taxpayer *n* [C] any person or organisation that is liable to pay tax: *Taxpayers will pay more to subsidise the development of alternative energy sources.*

Unit 13 Communication

correspondence *n* [U] writing, receiving and answering letters: *I'm catching up on my correspondence.* – correspond *v* [I]

information technology abbreviation **IT** *n* [C] the technology of processing, storing or transmitting data by electronic means: *Information technology has revolutionised all aspects of management.*

mobile *n* [C] a wireless telephone: *The introduction of colour screens and digital imaging have made mobiles even more essential.* Synonyms cell phone *n* [C] *AmE*

overload n [C] an excessive quantity of something: *You may be overwhelmed by the overload of information that is available on the net.* – overload v [I]

prioritise v [T] to put things in the order of importance so that you can deal with the most important things first: *Prioritising your work will help you to avoid backlogs.*

process v [T] to deal with information or documents: *All the data is processed on the server.* – process n [C]

product recall n [C] a situation where a defective product is withdrawn from the market and returned to the manufacturer: *Product recalls of children's toys are now very rare.*

text messaging n [U] a system which allows short text messages to be communicated by telephone: *Text messaging is far more popular than voice calls.* Synonyms SMS (Short Message Service) n [C]

white-collar adj employees who work in offices: *White-collar jobs are moving abroad.*

Unit 14 Logistics

distribution n [U] the arrangements and activities required in order to get goods from the manufacturer to the consumer: *Distribution is organised via a product list.*

finished goods n [plural] goods or products that are ready to be sold on to consumers: *We keep close track of the stock levels of our finished goods.*

freight n [U] the transportation of goods by air, sea, rail or road: *All freight is paid by the customer.* – freight v [T] Collocations *air-freight, freight car (AmE), freight train, freight forward*

grey marketing n [U] selling products without the authorisation of the trademark owner: *Any authorised dealers who resort to grey marketing will be immedaitely suspended.*

haulage n [U] the business of transporting goods by road or railway: *We are a haulage and warehousing company based in Poland.* Collocations *road-haulage*

loading bay n [C] the area in a factory or warehouse where goods are loaded for transport: *When a truck arrives at the loading bay an employee registers the delivery.*

pilot v [T] to test a new idea or product: *We are piloting new ways to improve our supply chain management.* Synonyms test v [T] trial v [T]

raw materials n [plural] materials such as minerals and hydrocarbons which are used in a production process: *Securing long term supplies of raw materials is critical.*

ship v [T] to move goods from one place to another: *This order is being shipped to Puerto Rico.* – shipment n [U] – shipping n [U] - ship n [C] Synonyms deliver v [T]

supply chain n [C] the interactions between the suppliers, manufacturers and distributors when making and selling a product: *Information technology has changed the dynamics of the supply chain* Collocations *supply chain management*

Unit 15 Innovation

achievement n [C] something that you succeed in doing by your own efforts: *Designing the first laptop computer was one of his greatest achievements.* – achieve v [T] – achiever n [C]

borderline n [C] the point at which one thing ends and another begins: *Many products fall into the borderline between different product categories* – borderline adj

breakthrough n [C] an important new discovery: *The iMac was a major breakthrough in computer design.* Collocations *make a breakthrough*

business practices n [plural] the methods used to conduct business: *The company is running a scheme to encourage best business practices.*

design v [T] to make a drawing or plan of something that will be made: *At the moment she's designing a new range of furniture to be used in schools.* – design n [C] – designer n [C] – designer adj Collocations *designer goods, designer label, designer ware,*

feature n [C] an important part of something: *The programme has a number of interesting new features.* – feature v [T] Synonyms characteristic n [C] Collocations *product features, special features*

generic adj a product that does not have a trademark:
Generic drugs sell at a much lower price.

mass-production adj produced in large quantities: *Many companies have moved their mass-production overseas to cheaper markets.* – mass-produce v [T] – mass-production n [U]

prototype n [C] the first form that a new design takes: *The prototype has revealed areas where the design can be improved.*

Glossary test

1 _____ profit is always calculated without deducting taxes and other charges.

  A Full   B Net
  C Whole   D Gross

2 The latest technology represents a major _____.

  A borderline   B breakdown
  C breakthrough D boundary

3 _____ have to evaluate the risks involved in setting up a business.

  A Suppliers   B Entrepreneurs
  C Regulators   D Managers

4 Four companies have announced that they will submit _____ for the project.

  A demands   B bids
  C subsidies   D quotas

5 _____ your staff means allowing them to make their own decisions.

  A Appraising   B Screening
  C Enforcing   D Empowering

6 We're having trouble filling the positions because of the _____ of skilled workers.

  A surplus   B reduction
  C shortage   D wealth

7 Our legal department has ensured that all our products are protected by _____.

  A infringement   B copycat
  C copyright   D legislation

8 The supply _____ brings together manufacturers, distributors and retailers.

  A link   B chain
  C channel   D line

9 The judge has awarded the company $15m in _____.

  A losses   B damages
  C charges   D bills

10 Detailed _____ of the accounts has revealed several suspicious transactions.

  A analysis   B data
  C facts   D figures

11 _____ our back-office work to an overseas supplier would definitely be cheaper.

  A Outsourcing   B Downsizing
  C Appointing   D Locating

12 R&D have asked us to file an application to _____ our new plasma technology.

  A trademark   B patent
  C brand   D record

13 You should always _____. That way you can do the most important work first.

  A rank   B prioritise
  C upgrade   D process

14 Falling sales in the US are bound to affect the company's _____.

  A currency   B bottom line
  C liabilities   D productivity

15 We'll need an additional _____ from the bank to cover our purchases.

  A expense   B account
  C loan   D debt

16 Why don't you _____ more work to the trainees?

  A subordinate B unload
  C delegate   D arrange

17 Only authorised _____ can carry out repairs under warranty.

  A wholesalers B carriers
  C dealers   D traders

18 This year's balance _____ shows that the company is clearly on the road to recovery.

  A form   B sheet
  C account   D book

19 Companies wishing to _____ for the project should follow the standard procedures.

  A tender   B offer
  C supply   D propose

20 On your _____ you should remember to print your name below your signature.

  A resumé   B CV
  C cover letter D application form

21 _____ between firms are like marriages: not always successful.

  A Acquisitions B Takeovers
  C Bids   D Mergers

22 Simple _____ such as data entry are given to junior employees.

  A tasks   B paperwork
  C assignments D missions

23 ComSoft has agreed to _____ us with the latest software.

A offer   B deliver
C supply   D sell

24 _____ allow company directors to buy shares at a preferential price.

A Severance deals   B Pension plans
C Pay packages   D Stock options

25 Cost-cutting and outsourcing will be the main focus of our _____ in the coming years.

A process   B objective
C strategy   D outlook

26 Distribution plays an important role in the _____ mix.

A advertising   B marketing
C selling   D promoting

27 If we used low-paid overseas workers we'd cut our _____ dramatically.

A profits   B costs
C margins   D income

28 Using cheaper components could result in considerable _____.

A winnings   B savings
C reductions   D decreases

29 _____ like rent are still taking up too much of our budget.

A Investments   B Overheads
C Earnings   D Taxes

30 With all these new orders it's going to be difficult to keep up with the _____.

A demand   B supply
C provisions   D volume

31 They have reported a second quarter _____ of £12m.

A lack   B loss
C reduction   D decline

32 The SEC is the official _____ for all US stock market trading.

A accountant   B dealer
C regulator   D broker

33 Mr Jackson has been _____ to our Swiss office for the next six months.

A assigned   B selected
C recruited   D hired

34 Most member states of the EU have adopted the Euro as the single _____.

A currency   B money
C cash   D exchange

35 Legislation against counterfeiting has always proved difficult to _____.

A empower   B enforce
C allow   D install

36 _____ designer clothing is openly sold in many markets.

A Dud   B Fraud
C Fake   D False

37 European farmers receive EU _____ for certain agricultural production.

A subsidies   B quotas
C tariffs   D lobbies

38 I love the new phones. They have some great new _____.

A features   B points
C characters   D items

39 Successful _____ will be asked to complete a series of tests in June.

A applications   B applicants
C appointments   D interviews

40 The _____ office is where all the administrative follow up is done.

A front   B back
C head   D corner

41 TransCargo is the _____ leader with operations all over Europe.

A industry   B induustrialist
C industrial   D industrious

42 It's too big a project for one company. Only a _____ can handle it.

A subsidiary   B corporation
C bureaucracy   D consortium

43 The biggest _____ we face is from cheap competition.

A asset   B weakness
C strength   D threat

44 Sourcing supplies of the necessary _____ will make manufacturing expensive.

A reserves   B real estate
C stock   D raw materials

45 The aim is to reduce the number of employees on the _____ by ten per cent.

A payroll   B bottom line
C department   D personnel

Grammar reference

Present simple and continuous

The present simple has the following uses.

- regular events and processes
  *We usually **start** the week with a team meeting.*
  *We **don't** actually **produce** the goods in the UK.*

  > **Key words**
  >
  > *a week / month / year, always, ever, never, often, rarely, seldom, sometimes, usually*

- facts that will not change
  *Our company **manufactures** mobile phones.*
  *We **use** suppliers in Singapore.*
- timetables and scheduled events
  *When **does** the plane **leave**?*
  *The conference **starts** at 9:30 am.*
- newspaper headlines
  *Interest rates **rise** again.*
  *Wagner **leaves** RDS board.*

The present continuous has the following uses.

- things happening now
  *We**'re setting up** a new office in Madrid.*
  *I**'m** just **looking** for your email now.*

  > **Key words**
  >
  > *now, at the moment, currently*

- temporary situations
  *She**'s attending** a training course this week.*
  *I**'m not travelling** in the region at the moment.*
- future arrangements
  *Where **are** you **meeting** them on Friday?*
  *We**'re not seeing** them until next week.*

The continuous is usually not used with the following stative verbs.

- verbs of emotion
  appreciate, dislike, hate, like, prefer, want
- verbs of thought
  believe, forget, know, mean, think, realise, recognise, remember, understand
- verbs of the senses
  appear, feel, hear, see, seem, smell, taste
- verbs of ownership
  have, need, own, want

Some verbs can be used with either the simple or continuous but with a change of meaning.

*I **think** the design looks good. (opinion)*
*We**'re thinking** about the design. (considering)*
*I **see** your point. (understanding)*
*I**'m seeing** him tomorrow. (meeting)*
*I **work** for Siemens. (permanent job)*
*I**'m working** for KPMG. (temporary contract)*

Articles

The indefinite article has the following uses.

- non-specific singular countable nouns
  *I've just been given **a** company car.*
  *There's **a** good course on management in May.*
- jobs and nouns of nationality
  *He's **a** sales manager.*
  *It's a Dutch firm but the director is **a** German.*

The definite article has the following uses.

- nouns already mentioned or specified
  ***The** computer system cost ten thousand dollars.*
  ***The** course I'm doing is excellent.*
- nouns that are one of a kind
  the world, the internet, the OECD
- groups of people
  the Japanese, the unemployed, the workers
- the superlative form of adjectives
  *She's **the best** manager I've ever worked for.*
  *Fear isn't **the most** effective way to motivate staff.*

No article is needed with the following.

- proper names
  *Our headquarters are in **Hamburg**.*
  *He works for **Apple Computer** in California.*
- general plural and uncountable nouns
  ***People** are spending more and more.*
  *It's important that **objectives** are achievable.*
  ***Business** is good these days.*
- certain abstract nouns
  *She works in **finance**.*
  ***Fear** can be a good motivator.*
  *He doesn't respond well to **criticism**.*
- in certain prepositional phrases
  at home, at university, at work, by train

Future forms

will + infinitive has the following uses.

- predictions
  *The budget **won't be** finalised until next week.*
  ***Will** the report **be** ready in time?*

- spontaneous decisions or offers
  *There's no answer so **I'll try** again later.*
  *Don't worry, **I'll make** all the arrangements.*

- things that we want to make happen
  ***I'll finish** everything before I leave on holiday.*
  *Don't worry. **We'll make** our targets this year.*

will + present perfect has the following uses.

- events completed before a future time
  *The meeting **will have finished** by six o'clock.*
  *How long **will** you **have been** here by then?*

going to + verb has the following uses.

- personal intentions
  *We're **going to look** for a new business partner.*
  *What **are** you **going to do** about it?*

- predictions
  *The new product's **going to win** us market share.*
  *It's **not going to be** easy with the dollar so low.*

> ### will or going to?
>
> Often either verb phrase is possible with no change in meaning.
>
> *I think it'**ll rain** later.*
>
> *I think it's **going to rain** later.*
>
> However, *will* usually has a more spontaneous feel, whereas *going to* suggests present evidence.
>
> *We're late so we'**re not going to hit** our deadline.*
>
> *He's late but I'm sure he'**ll be** here soon.*

The present simple has the following uses.

- timetabled events
  *The plane **leaves** at 7:30 am tomorrow.*

The present continuous has the following uses.

- events arranged for a certain time
  *We're **meeting** the suppliers next Monday.*

Modal verbs have the following uses.

- predictions
  *We **might have to** lower our prices in future.*
  *It **could be** a difficult strategy meeting tomorrow.*

Present perfect and past simple

The present perfect has the following uses.

- changes that affect the present
  *The remuneration committee's **finished** its report.*
  ***Have** the shareholders **been informed** yet?*

- situations that started in the past and continue
  *CEOs **have been receiving** huge rises for years.*
  *We've **been looking** at the issue of executive pay.*

- show duration
  *I **haven't been promoted** for five years.*
  *He's **been** the chairman since 2002.*

> ### Key words
>
> *for* (with periods of time) and *since* (with points in time: e.g. times, days, dates, etc.), *already, yet, just, ever, never, recently, lately, in the last, today, this week / month / year*

The past simple has the following uses.

- finished actions and events
  *She **worked** here for five years.* (not now)
  ***Did** you **meet** her at the conference?*

- definite or finished time periods
  *I **joined** the company in 2003.*
  *They **launched** the product two years ago.*
  *When **did** you **go** to Dubai?*

> ### Key words
>
> days, months, years, times, *yesterday, ago, last week / month / year*

> ### Perfect or past?
>
> Without a time adverbial the choice of perfect or past can make news sound either very new or old.
>
> *They've **brought out** a new product.* (recently)
>
> *They **brought out** a new product.* (some time ago)
>
> *They've **published** a report on CEO pay.* (new)
>
> *They **published** a report on CEO pay.* (old news)

The perfect often introduces a topic, whereas the past is used for further details.

A *Has the report **been published** yet?*

B *Yes, it **has**. I **saw** it last week.*

A *What **was** in it? Anything exciting?*

B *Nothing too shocking. But it **did make** several references to the generous pay rise the board **awarded** themselves last year.*

Modal verbs

All modal verbs can show degrees of likelihood.

- certainty
  The new factory **will** damage the environment.
  That **must** be the best solution.

- probability
  The loan **should** secure the project's future.
  Tighter laws **would** protect the rainforest.
  Higher oil prices **ought to** hit exports.

- possibility
  We **could** ask investors for more money.
  They **might** pull out if they don't get the loan.
  Public demonstrations **may** make a difference.

Modal verbs also have the following uses.

- intentions
  We **won't** go ahead without the loan.
  We **might not** go ahead without the guarantees.

- obligation, necessity or prohibition
  You **ought to** get permission first.
  Companies **mustn't** be allowed to drill there.
  We **have to** get a visa for visiting Lebanon now.
  You **can't smoke** in restaurants in the USA.

- lack of obligation or necessity
  We **don't have to** get an import licence.
  You **needn't** do it now. We'll do it later.

- permission
  Can we import directly into that market?
  May we send you a copy of our brochure?

- advice or recommendation
  You **should** visit the rainforest. It's beautiful.
  We **ought to** increase our spending on PR.

- suggestions
  We **should** invite the press to visit the site.
  Couldn't we offer them a better discount?
  Shall I give them a call?

- requests
  Could you email a copy of the report?
  Would you ask her to give me a call?
  May I use your mobile for a moment?

Past modal verbs have the following uses.

- talk about alternative possibilities
  With better research we **could have made** the product more reliable.
  With better training our staff **would have coped** better with the problems that came up.

- give advice after events have happened
  You **should have done** more testing.
  You **ought to have understood** the market better.

- show degrees of likelihood
  Smaller handsets **would have made** the phones more appealing to young people.
  Launching later **might have allowed** our competitors to beat us to market.

Comparatives and superlatives

Comparatives are formed as follows.

- add -er for one-syllable adjectives
  Consumers are **harder** to reach nowadays.
  Many products are **cheaper** than ten years ago.

- add -ier for adjectives ending with -y
  People are **busier** than ever before.
  I prefer the other design. It looks **trendier**.

- use more / less for multi-syllable adjectives
  Brands are **more powerful** in today's economy.
  Our last product was **more expensive**.

- irregular comparative forms (good, bad, far)
  We're **better** at identifying our customer now.
  The figures are far **worse** than expected.
  Call me if you need any **further** information.
  The new office is **farther** from the city centre.

Superlatives are formed as follows.

- add the -est for one-syllable adjectives
  A brand was **the simplest** stamp of quality.
  The deadline was **the shortest** we've worked to.

- add the -iest for adjectives ending with -y
  Building a brand is not **the easiest** thing to do.
  It's **the funniest** campaign I've ever seen.

- use the most / least for multi-syllable adjectives
  Many of **the most expensive** brands are copied.
  It's **the least successful** campaign we've ever had.

- irregular superlative forms (good, bad)
  Having **the best** features is no longer enough.
  It's **the worst** slump in advertising for years.

Adverbs have the following forms.

- add more / less for comparative adverbs
  TV advertising reaches people **more efficiently**.
  They can do the same but far **less expensively**.

- add the most / least for superlative adverbs
  Ms Klein's book made the point **most forcefully**.
  It's our **most successfully** marketed product.

(not) as ... as

- all comparisons can be made in two ways
  Image is **more important than** quality.
  Quality **isn't as important as** image.

Conditionals

Conditional sentences are formed as follows.

- Type 1: *if* + present tense, present tense or modal
  If companies **outsource,** **they reduce** *costs.*
  If we **don't do** *it, we* **might lose** *market share.*

- Type 2: *if* + past tense, *would / could* + verb
  If we **cut** *jobs, the unions* **would fight** *the move.*
  Could *we* **save** *money if we* **went** *offshore?*

- Type 3: *if* + *had* + verb, *would / could have* + verb
  If we'd **known,** *we* **wouldn't have done** *it.*
  We **could have stopped** *it if we'd* **known** *about it.*

Conditional type 1 has the following uses.

- cause and effect
  If you **reduce** *costs, you* **increase** *margins.*
  People **work** *harder if you* **pay** *them more.*

- predict consequences of likely situations
  Morale **will fall** *if we* **lay** *people off.*
  We'll **lose** *sales if we* **don't reduce** *the price.*

- request action in the event of a likely situation
  Call *me if you* **get** *any more information.*
  Let *me know if you* **have** *any problems.*

Conditional type 2 has the following uses.

- cause and effect in the past (not true now)
  If I **called** *him, he* **wouldn't answer** *the phone.*
  I'd **switch** *my phone off if we* **were** *in a meeting.*

- predict consequences of unlikely situations
  There **would be** *a backlash if they* **left** *the USA.*
  If overheads **weren't** *so high we'd* **invest** *more.*

Conditional type 3 has the following uses.

- hypothetical situations in the past
  I'd **have gone** *to China if I* **hadn't had** *children.*
  If we'd **known,** *we* **wouldn't have done** *it.*
  I **would have called** *you if I'd* **had** *your number.*

Some conditional sentences mix types 1 and 2.

I **wouldn't need** *a translator if I'd* **studied** *at school.*
If we'd **gone** *offshore, our costs* **would be** *lower now.*

Adjectives and adverbs

Adjectives have the following uses.

- before nouns
  There was a **sharp** *rise in profits last year.*
  We saw a **sudden** *increase in trading yesterday.*

- after stative verbs such as *be, become, seem,* etc.
  The falling share price could be **serious.**
  Investors are becoming **nervous** *about the market.*

Adverbs have the following uses.

- after verbs
  CEO pay has risen **sharply** *in the last few years.*
  Their accounts were audited **recently.**

- before an adjective or adverb
  Bosses are getting **increasingly** *lavish pay-offs.*
  Prices have been rising **fairly** *slowly this year.*

Some adverbs have irregular forms.

The scandal hit the company **hard.**
We'll have to move **fast** *before the press get the story.*
She arrived **late** *for the meeting.*
The company hasn't been doing **well** *this year.*

Relative pronouns

Defining relative clauses define or differentiate the person or thing they refer to. They have the following forms.

- who, which or that
  Simon is the person **who** *has most experience.*
  It's the interviews **that / which** *take time.*

- no pronoun (if the object of the verb is in the clause)
  The people **(who)** *we interviewed were good.*
  They ignored the advice **(that)** *we gave them.*

- whose
  We ignored those **whose** *applications were late.*

Non-defining relative clauses only give extra information and do not define what they refer to. They have the following forms.

- who, which, whom, that, whose (within commas)
  The interviews, **which** *were held at the hotel, lasted exactly thirty minutes.*

Gerunds and infinitives

Gerunds have the following uses.

- after prepositions
  He joined us after **working** *for a competitor.*
  I'm not interested in **buying** *things on the net.*

- as a noun
  Registering *as a seller only takes a few minutes.*
  The **policing** *of the site is done by the users.*

- after certain expressions
  There's no point **bidding** *now. It's been sold.*

- after certain verbs
  We've just finished **preparing** the new website.

Infinitives have the following uses.

- after adjectives
  The website is very easy **to use**.
  It's important **to preserve** the community feeling.

- showing purpose
  Some people quit jobs **to become** eBay traders.

- after certain verbs
  Many rivals aim **to build** bigger websites.

- after certain verbs + object
  We asked him **to present** the figures next week.

Some verbs can be followed by either a gerund or an infinitive with no difference in meaning.

I prefer **buying** CDs on the internet.

I prefer **to buy** CDs on the internet.

Some can be followed by either a gerund or an infinitive but with a difference in meaning.

We **stopped selling** the old designs. (what is stopped?)

We **stopped to get** a coffee. (reason for stopping?)

I **remember seeing** it in the papers. (refers to past)

Remember to send the report. (refers to future)

Reported speech

Speech can be reported using the same words as the speaker used.

- with the same tense
  He says he**'ll send** an email to confirm the date.

- changing the tense (when reporting verb in past)
  She said she**'d called** him several times.
  He said they **were having** problems with email.

- with modal verbs (which never change form)
  He says he **can finish** the report by Friday.

Speech can be reported by summarising what the speaker said rather than using the same words. (See infinitives opposite.)

- with certain reporting verbs + infinitive
  He **refused to take** a laptop with him on the trip.
  We **promised to cut** the amount of paperwork.

- with certain reporting verbs + object + infinitive
  She **asked me to copy** you in on the report.
  They **warned us not to open** any suspicious files.

- with certain reporting verbs + gerund
  He **admitted reading** work emails on holiday.

Passives

Passives have the following uses.

- when the agent is unknown or unimportant
  The stock **was delivered** to us this morning.
  The shelves **haven't been upgraded** yet.
  The tags **can be switched off** by a kill switch.

- systems and processes
  The stock **is scanned** as it enters the warehouse.
  The figures **are being finalised** at the moment.

- formal reports and notices
  It **is recommended** that smart tags be introduced.
  The issue **was raised** by the company's auditors.

- reporting unconfirmed information
  The CEO **is said to be** in favour of smart tags.
  They **are thought to be** cheaper than barcodes.

Audioscripts

Unit 1   **Listening** page 13

Jeff Hynes

Well, this is it! This, is the company as such. I set it up a year ago and we are still subcontracting most of our activities out to other smaller independent suppliers. My job involves liaising and dealing with all the other companies we use, as well as co-ordinating the work of my five project managers here in the office.

Harry Wilson

Running a multinational like this is a challenging but rewarding job. I oversee every aspect of company policy and practice. Of course, not everyone works directly for me, that would be impossible, but you could say that since I took over three years ago I am ultimately responsible for the 15,000 employees worldwide.

Karl-Heinz Egonolf

My job entails dealing with the external auditors as well as overseeing the quarterly reports. I have asked for more staff because the ten accountants who work under me are worked flat out here at head office.

Jill Black

I'm in charge of 25 people who take phone orders all day for a number of different companies. I'm responsible for recruiting and training all staff members. I report to our client companies who use our services and I'm also responsible for contacting and meeting new clients.

Mary Fitzsimmons

When I took over the department eight years ago our main activity was writing the in-house journals but the main part of the job, nowadays, involves dealing with the press. Our whole communication strategy is based on keeping the public informed by sending out press releases outlining our policies and intentions. The department employs a staff of about 15 but I'm also in charge of a team of 20 freelance writers we employ on a fairly regular basis.

Unit 2   **Listening 1** page 19

In my department we set clear goals and targets for a fixed period of time. We try to make it worth people's time to reach those targets through our performance-related bonus scheme. We have regular meetings to see if everyone is on track during that period of time and at the end we have an appraisal meeting to evaluate the work that has been done. Naturally, if we find that the deadlines were too tight or things didn't get done because of factors beyond our control, we sometimes adjust schedules to more realistic time frameworks.

I like to get in early before the rest of my staff and design the daily work schedule of each team member. That way I feel very much in control and that I have a hand in every task. My staff know that I like to be involved in every decision and they always consult me when they run into problems. We've been working successfully like this for years in the company and I find that it reassures people to have a strong leader heading operations. They have their own responsibilities, naturally, but when it comes to the important decisions it's me who makes them.

In my view, one of the most important things to learn as a manager is how to delegate. That way you get people to feel that they are a part of a team and it gives them a real sense of belonging and that, in turn, generates responsibility towards the organisation. So you've got to give employees the space they need so they can take initiatives and really move things forward. If you've recruited the right people for the job then you should let them get on with it!

Unit 2   **Listening 2** page 21

One

A   Hi, Sally. I've been looking for you.
B   Oh, hi Tom. What can I do for you?
A   We're falling behind schedule on the new project and I was wondering whether you could do some overtime this week?
B   Sure, how much do you need?

Two

A   Alan, it's Michelle. I'm on holiday next week so I'm doing my monthly report early. I don't suppose you could give me your report early as well, could you?
B   Shouldn't be a problem. I'll do it tomorrow.

Three

A   So, Peter, we need to cut costs by at least ten per cent?

B It looks that way, yes.
A Would you mind putting together a brief report identifying a few areas where we can make some savings?
B OK. When do you need it by?

Unit 2 Decision page 22

For me, the whole story of Carlos Ghosn and the Nissan turnaround is one of the most fascinating cases in international management and leadership that I've seen recently. Because here you have a brash, cost-cutting Renault executive taking on a key assignment in a country with very different business traditions and very specific ways of doing business. And right from the word go, Carlos Ghosn makes it clear that he isn't going to play the game by the rule book. Now that's pretty brave to say the least – revolutionary might be a better word. And what's even more amazing is that it actually worked! He succeeds in putting through a cost-cutting plan that no one at Nissan would have dared to present; he restructured the whole company, he eliminated jobs and even destroyed the long-standing relationship with suppliers. And what reaction did he get? He became a star of the Japanese business world – and a role model for the salaryman; the man who saved Nissan! So it's a real success story and one that I think illustrates how difficult it is to predict whether or not a particular style of leadership is the right one. And when Ghosn first arrived in Japan, I don't think many people thought that he would be staying for very long.

Unit 3 Listening 1 page 24

Well, all business organisations need to have a framework to help them to analyse their current position and then to use that information to help them to prepare for the future. There are many different ways that they can do this. Probably the best known is what's called the SWOT analysis. This very neatly divides the problem into four areas. It's normally represented as a square divided into four parts. At the top you have the S for strengths and the W for weaknesses. And then on the bottom line you have the O for opportunities and then T for threats. The idea is that if you analyse a business using these four criteria, then you should have the basic information to allow you to map out what the best strategy might be.

Under strengths, you would put the things that it does well, and then under weaknesses, the things that it doesn't do quite so well. That leaves two spaces: one for opportunities that the company is in a position to exploit, and one for threats – the dangers that it will be exposed to in its markets in the future.

Unit 3 Listening 2 page 28

Naomi: Hi, Bruce. It's Naomi here. I'm calling about the conference in Shanghai. We're going to have to make some changes.

Bruce: Hi, Naomi. OK, hang on, let me get a pen. Right, fire away.

Naomi: I don't think the Yangtze Garden will be big enough. We're going to need a centre that can seat at least 600.

Bruce: That many? Any suggestions?

Naomi: The Mandarin Palace Center will be free that day. I've already spoken to them and I'm meeting the conference manager tomorrow. It'll mean increasing the registration fee by $50 though.

Bruce: That won't be a problem. Anything else?

Naomi: Alasdair Ross can't do the morning session as his plane doesn't land until 9:30, so I've arranged things with Jimmy Tan and they're going to switch slots. Also, Milan University say they're sending Carla Marisco because Professor Bertoni can't make it. But the talk will be the same.

Bruce: Fine. Make those changes and I'll inform everyone at my end.

Unit 3 Decision page 30

This is the classic dilemma for any company that relies heavily on one customer group. It's clear that they have to innovate and try to rejuvenate the image of their bikes to try to attract new customers. That's not easy to do because Harley Davidson already has a very strong and quite specific image. So they have had to be very careful not to turn off their existing customers by moving too far towards what their Japanese competition is offering.

What the company in fact did was introduce new Harley Davidson models like the V-Rod to provide a more exciting product line while, at the same time, developing the Buell Blast bikes to give younger riders a chance to buy into the Harley experience. The problem's been that Buell is not that well-known, so sales have been quite modest (only about four per cent of Harley Davidson revenue) but it has given the company a chance to promote itself through rider instruction programmes and to draw in a new group of customers.

Among the other options that Harley is considering is overseas expansion. But the problem here is that in some countries their bikes aren't certified – in Taiwan for example – and entering the Chinese market is going to be very difficult without making an alliance with a local manufacturer, and they won't do that until they are sure that they've found a partner who can be trusted with the Harley brand.

Unit 4   Preview page 34

Brad Jefferson

Yeah, I guess you could call me successful. I mean I drive a BMW 740 and my home is worth about $4m. Not bad for a guy who's just 35 years old. I knew what I wanted right from the start and stayed focused until I got it. When I first started with the company, I worked on average 80 hours a week. When I became CEO, last year, I slowed down a bit to between 60 and 80 hours. You see, this is a work- and wealth-obsessed culture ... we think work 24/7 – 24 hours a day, 7 days a week. It's normal. (laughs) I think it's worth it – after all I earn around $3 million in salary a year plus bonuses, so I can't complain.

Anne Lee Chang

I've been living in the valley for three years now. I came here to take up a post of senior manager at a software company. I was tempted by the fabulous pay deal, you know, the $3m, 'couldn't say no', deal. You know, the challenge of being a woman, an Asian-American and all that, and also I love my job, my lifestyle, my jaguar sports car. I knew it would mean an average of 60 or so hours a week when I accepted the job – on a good week that is, but I'm young, I'm 32, so I can take it. The downside, of course, is you have to sacrifice your personal life. There are 43 million single women in 'the valley' and around 36 million single men.

Unit 4   Listening 1 page 37

Part one

Well most CEOs' earnings sound exceptionally high because those figures are based on what we refer to as total compensation ... in other words ... salary and various bonuses, of course, and then, more importantly, what they are actually worth in terms of share value. And it is often this share value that makes the figures so very impressive. Take, for example, the highest paid CEO in the US in 2003. This was the head of Tenet Healthcare, a guy called Jeffery Barbakow. His total compensation for the period was $116,683,000. Can you believe it, one year's earnings? $116,683,000, I mean that's a phenomenal amount of money but his salary and bonuses for 2003 amounted to only $5,530,000, which is a reasonable salary by US standards at the time. His shares, however, were valued at $111,050,000 and this is what drove up his total. And then he picked up another $250,000 in other fees somewhere along the way.

Part two

Now, you see, obviously some people, even some shareholders, would accept that kind of compensation because it is accepted wisdom that making the managers part-owners of the company, through shares and stock options, is the best form of incentive or motivation.

That is all very fine, but what that theory fails to take into consideration is that market fluctuations mean that share value can at times be very different from their original value, and management could even encourage this in the short term in order to sell their shares before the market changes or falls again.

So you see, the heart of the problem seems to be motivation, and it's rather simple if you treat managers in the same way as other employees. They are generally keen to reach objectives or goals set out for them, because they know that when they are appraised or evaluated they'll get their bonuses or increases in salaries based on whether they met those goals or not. If company bosses have to come up with the goods in order to get their salaries, actually earn them ... problem solved, basically. They could be promoted on the basis of company performance – and I don't mean if share prices increase due to a general rise in the stock market – I mean if the company actually outperforms other companies in the same sector. Not even the toughest shareholders would object to that!

Unit 4   Listening 2 page 39

A How's it going with the Titanium project? Are you going to be able to meet the deadline?

B Possibly. We were behind schedule last month. We've almost caught up but the deadline's still too tight. Could we extend it?

A That might be difficult. What's the problem?

B We've had real technical problems. The whole network shut down last week for two days.

A Well, I can maybe negotiate a two-day extension. Leave it with me, I'll see what I can do. Will you still come in on budget?

B Not now. The network problems have meant we've had to contract a lot of the work out to meet the deadline, so there'll be an overspend on the data processing. It shouldn't be too much though.

Unit 4 Decision page 40

The dilemma here is the age-old 'value for money' problem, isn't it? With people, of course, there are no guarantees. Look at the outgoing CEO. I'm sure he looked like a one-way bet three years ago! That's why I personally wouldn't go for John Creed. Of course, he would inspire confidence in the market and the share price would certainly go up in the short term, but like I said, there's no guarantee. So why risk all that money on an unknown outsider when you have a proven internal candidate?

I'm not saying that David Preston will cost that much less in the long run – it's unrealistic to think you'd save on the COO's salary. Companies that made similar decisions soon realised that the CEO needs someone to look after the day-to-day running of the business. He won't be able to do his job properly if there isn't a COO. That makes him a very expensive candidate too. As for increasing dividends, well ... personally, I think shareholders shouldn't be too influenced by this and consider their long-term investment in the company.

So what about Ms Sweetman? Well, she's obviously going to cost less. It's a good idea to lower expectations in times of trouble, so she got that right. I also think that, even if she isn't able to reduce staff costs easily, maybe she can improve services and efficiency. So, she's the one I'd go for.

For the moment, women still have more realistic salary expectations than men. Now is the time to put them at the top! I'm sure the shareholders would agree! Even if it means no more unrealistic dividends, steady, long-term growth is much more important.

Unit 5 Listening 1 page 42

Thank you for inviting me today to speak about the OECD and its work. Let me first begin by telling you a little about its origins. The Organisation for Economic Cooperation and Development was established to help countries develop their economies after World War II. It soon became a meeting place, or forum, for the governments of the more economically developed countries of the world to discuss, compare and improve their economic and social policies.

As an international organisation, the OECD is funded by contributions from member country governments. In return, the OECD provides advice, detailed statistics and data on a wide range of subjects including economic performance, projected growth rates for different countries, as well as social policy, education, trade, agriculture, the environment and development.

In the era of globalisation, with the new key objectives of sustainable development and poverty reduction, the OECD has shifted more of its work to the economic development of other countries by trying to share with them the lessons – both positive and negative – of the OECD's experience with economic and social development. In today's talk I'm going to be looking at the role of the OECD in Latin America's developing economies ...

Unit 5 Listening 2 page 47

One

A Hi, Andrès, it's Shirley here. Have you got a second?

B Sure. How can I help?

A I was wondering if you'd received any news about those new orders that we were expecting for next month?

B Well, in fact I just got confirmation from Brazil this morning. They now say they want two hundred units by the end of the month. That's fifty more than we were expecting.

A Two hundred! Wow! That's not going to be easy. It'll mean that we'll have to put production staff on to extra time and maybe even subcontract some of the work.

Two

A Hey, David, I don't seem to be able to connect to the network. Do you have any idea what's going on?

B Yeah. I just called the IT department to find out and they told me the entire computer network will be down for the rest of the day.

A Did they tell you what the problem was?

B Apparently there's a virus attack going on and it's caused the whole system to close down automatically. They say it will be several hours before they can fix it.

A It couldn't happen at a worse time for me. I'm supposed to send my monthly report out today.

Well, in many ways the Camisea project has been, at least so far, a case study in how not to manage a development project in an environmentally sensitive area of the world like the Amazon. Right from the start we've seen a long list of all kinds of mistakes. Just to mention a few: insufficient guidelines on construction procedures, poor quality control of the work on the ground, a lack of communication with the local people and, perhaps most importantly, no evaluation of the impact of the project on local communities and the environment. So I think the lesson to be learned here is that it is not possible to proceed with a project of this sort if you are not going to respect the international guidelines and the accepted international standards for construction and development inside a sensitive area such as the rainforest. I don't think we can lay the blame for all this with any specific group involved in the project, but I think it is very disappointing to see that the work of international institutions like the World Bank, which have laid down precise guidelines for exactly this type of project, has not been taken into account. What will happen in the long run? I expect the project will go ahead, especially as quite a lot of the work has already been completed. However, at least the work of environmental groups has meant that more attention is now being paid to minimising the damage that may result.

Brand strategy is the driving force behind a business, there's no doubt about it. Brands are what all businesses are trying to create and build on. Successful brands are a company's most valuable asset. You see, your brand is the unmistakable symbol for your products and services and to get that unmistakable symbol you need to make sure it has all the characteristics of a successful brand.

First of all, it needs to be distinctive, you know, it has to stand out in the crowd, not be easily confused with competing brands. Then, it needs to be easy to memorise, so complicated images, too many colours and sophisticated names are out.

The next thing is that the brand name must be easy to pronounce and, if possible, in several languages.

Your brand also has to fit the image of the product. I mean, there's no point in coming up with a wonderful concept if it doesn't have anything to do with the actual product.

Finally, it is important that the brand communicates the right emotional appeal to your target customer.

Once established, a successful brand will almost never let you down. Other things may change: positioning, packaging, whatever, but the brand will remain the same. Take for instance, Chanel's 'No 5' perfume. It is still the best-selling perfume in the world. Imagine, with all the competition that's out there – the thousands of perfumes that have come onto the market since its launch and there it still is – right at the top! A perfume named 'No 5'! Not very inspiring, you might think, but the brand is *Chanel*. The name speaks for itself. That's the power of a brand. Well, No 5 may have been helped a little by the famous remarks from Marilyn Monroe in the 60s when she said she slept in nothing but Chanel No 5. There's nothing like a celebrity endorsement to push up sales.

1   I think I'll opt for this one; after all, it's only just more expensive than the others.
2   Having looked at all the options, this one seems significantly better than the others.
3   I don't think we should offer this candidate the job, she's way too qualified for the position.
4   The new range didn't sell quite as well as we'd expected.
5   The first suggestion seems rather easier than the others. I'll go for that one.
6   I feel reasonably more comfortable with Jeremy's idea, if you don't mind.
7   We've looked at all the new sample designs and they're a lot better than the ones we had before.
8   This campaign is by far the most exciting one we've seen up to now.

This is an interesting case. Personally, I'd say both brands would have a very good chance of succeeding.

But if I had to make a choice, I suppose it would be cheaper and probably even safer to simply bring out a new fragrance which fits easily within the image of the existing range. Plus, of course, the target customer would be more willing to pay a high price for a fragrance and therefore fairly high promotional costs could be more easily justified.

However, in spite of all that, I think I'd go for launching a completely new brand with a newer and trendier image. It appears to be a far riskier choice but I suspect that in reality it's not quite as adventurous as it sounds. After all, once you've covered reasonably higher promotional costs, and you need to get that marketing campaign absolutely right, by the way, then you have access to a whole new market of younger customers. You might even save money on the packaging, as it doesn't require such expensive materials. But – and this is a big one – you have to be careful not to lose your base customers, and the new 'younger', probably cheaper, fragrance mustn't change the brand image of the established high-value products in the range.

It is doable but relatively difficult. Look at Chanel, it chose Vanessa Paradis to endorse its perfume 'Coco' in 1984 and she was a teenage pop star at the time, not at all adapted to the traditional Chanel image. But that opened up a huge new teenage market for Chanel and those customers have remained loyal to the brand ever since.

So yeah, I'd definitely go for the second option. Of course, as a brand consultant, my opinion may be just influenced by the fact that it is tremendously more challenging and interesting to create a new brand.

Unit 7 Listening 1 page 60

I think that by now most managers have realised that there are substantial savings to be made by outsourcing certain parts of their operations overseas. But having said that, you can't just start outsourcing everything that your company does. First of all, only certain types of work actually lend themselves to outsourcing – where there is no need for face-to-face contact and where a secure and reliable network connection is available. So that restricts things pretty much to IT, Human Resources, R&D and back-office work.

The second thing to remember is that there are a number of constraints you have to work with. The first of those is language – there's no point outsourcing if you don't have professional people at the other end who can speak your language. That's why offshoring today has centred on US and UK companies locating in countries like India and the Philippines where English is a part of the culture. Next comes the wage factor or 'differential' as it's called. If there isn't a substantial saving to be made here, then the risks simply outweigh the potential benefits. So I would say that if you can't get a 50 per cent saving here, then it won't be worth all the extra costs involved in transferring work abroad.

Then there are the risk factors that you have to look at. Political stability is certainly one of those. What will you do if there is a major problem in the country you have outsourced to? And there's also the question of protecting your assets – not giving away your trade secrets to partners who may use that knowledge to their own advantage. So yes, it's a complex decision and one where you have to weigh the advantages and drawbacks very carefully.

Unit 7 Listening 2 page 64

Part one

Int: Hello Régis. Perhaps you'd like to begin by telling us what company you work for?

Régis: I am working for Slash Support Ltd., a company that provides 24/7 worldwide support on IT products – network and telecommunications mainly.

Int: What exactly does your job involve?

Régis: I'm working in the Alcatel Voice team and we provide support for internet and telephone systems. When a customer has a problem with a system or wants some technical assistance, they get in touch with the support centre and our role is to solve the problem and answer any questions.

Int: Does the company employ mostly local people?

Régis: No, it's very hard to find people locally. Most of my colleagues aren't from Chennai itself. Companies such as Slash Support usually have to recruit at national level because it is not always easy to find local people with the necessary foreign language skills. Slash also hires trainees from Germany, France, and Latin America who come on short-term assignments. So, there is a good mix of local people and people from abroad.

Int: Was it difficult to adjust to working in a new environment?

Régis: Yeah. It was hard to adapt to the rhythm of work at the beginning. Here we do shifts which are ten hours long – from 8 am to 6 pm.

Int: That's a long day.

Régis: It is. And then, on top of that, during the first three months, I was also getting training every morning, so I was pretty tired when I got home in the evening!

Int: What are your Indian colleagues like, you know, in terms of age, education ... are they mostly male or female?

Régis: Most of my colleagues are from non-technical backgrounds. They have been hired for their language skills – not because of their technical abilities. One of them is even a lawyer by training. They are almost only men and mostly between 25 and 35 years old.

Int: And how are you settling in? Where are you living at the moment?

Régis: The company's been working with the US and Europe for some time now, so everyone's had time to adapt. It's more difficult to adapt outside work than in the office. I've been living with an Indian family, so I had to learn how to fit in with their lifestyle – but they're really kind and I've learned lots about Indian culture from them – more than if I'd stayed in a hotel, for example. I'm hoping to get my own apartment soon, though.

Part two

Int: How do you react when you hear people saying that Indian companies are 'stealing' jobs from Europe and the USA?

Régis: Today with globalisation, everybody is working together and competition is now worldwide. The first point to make is that it was the European and US companies that contacted the Indian companies. And that is completely understandable. Companies find the same skills at a cheaper price and with more flexibility. So, if it is interesting for the company, why shouldn't they take advantage of it? But one must not forget that it is not always that easy for a company to outsource to India and that it's not always a success. It may be true that some jobs have left Europe and the US, but other jobs have also been created, for instance, in companies which are specialised in helping businesses to make their outsourcing process a success.

I think this is only the beginning of the phenomenon, as many countries such as France, for example, have not really outsourced yet. This is a huge market and India seems to be leading the race. But some other countries are coming up as competitors and to keep its place, India will have to stay competitive. But its experience will be a big advantage.

Unit 7   Listening 3 page 65

One
A Oh, hi Maria. Have you got a minute? There's something I'd like to ask you.

B Well, sure. Is something the matter?

A Well, yes. Remember that job I told you I'd applied for? Well, they've asked me to come in for an interview next Monday. The problem is, I'm supposed to be working that day. What do you think I should do?

B Well, if I were you, I wouldn't say anything. Just tell your manager that you need to take the day off for personal reasons.

A But what if he asks me about my personal reasons?

Two
A We need to decide where we're going to hold the sales conference. Does anyone have any suggestions?

B Couldn't we do it in the same place as last year? It was perfect and it has all the facilities that we need.

A I know, but the only problem is they don't have enough rooms available for the whole week.

Three
A I have received another complaint about Bob Stewart. He's been coming in late for work again.

B Again! I thought you warned him about that just a couple of weeks ago?

A I did but it doesn't seem to make any difference.

B It can't go on like this. I really think that you should send him a written warning this time.

A You're right. I'll write to him tomorrow.

Four
A Have you seen the latest sales figures? They're down on last month.

B I know. We expected them to fall but not by that much. What do you think we can do about it?

A Why don't you call a meeting of all sales staff and make it absolutely clear to them that if they don't generate more business, there'll be no bonus this year.

B OK, let's try that. That might do the trick.

Five
A How long is it going to be before you finish drawing up the proposal?

B I don't think we'll have it ready before the end of next week at the earliest.

A That's not soon enough. We absolutely need to get it out by the end of this week.

B In that case it might be better to get some more people involved.

A It's a good idea but I'm afraid we can't afford it.

Six
A Is there any way we could change the schedule? We'll never have time to get through all this in one morning.

B That's going to be difficult, especially as we have another meeting immediately after lunch.

A Well, what about dealing with the most urgent matters first and just leaving the rest until later?

B Sounds good to me. We'll do that, then.

Unit 7 Decision page 66

Well, in this case there are a number of issues that have to be looked at. First, there is the question of business performance itself. Is it really going to be worthwhile for this company to take part of its business offshore? There's not much doubt there – it will be cheaper at least in the short-term. But there is a downside and that could produce some surprises for any company. The image of the company may well suffer as a result of a decision to offshore, and the potential impact of that is difficult to measure. We've already seen that sort of thing happening and some companies have even had to bring back work that they had outsourced. This, of course, could be made worse by union industrial action. Other problems down the line? Well, when you offshore a critical part of your business, you really have to have a fall-back strategy if something goes disastrously wrong. This could be what we call 'multi-shoring', where you have an alternative service provider in another country you can switch to if things go wrong. That way, if there is a major appreciation in wages or foreign currency, a dispute with your local provider or any sort of instability, you're not in danger. So you know, I think that if I were being asked to choose a destination for an outsourcing operation, I would advise the company to think very carefully about 'multi-shoring' – that way they can minimise the risks and transfer operations to another destination if something goes wrong.

Unit 8 Listening 1 page 68

We are very happy to announce that we achieved our sales forecasts of $700m last year. What's more, the cheaper costs of outsourcing to Indonesia for many of our parts was even more cost-effective than we'd hoped – reducing our manufacturing expenses by $30m – down to $70m. Outsourcing in Indonesia also generated significant savings of $10m in salaries. Therefore, gross profit is up at $840m. This is a trend we hope will continue into the next quarter and many more to come.

On the other hand, trading or operating profit fell slightly – but there are clear reasons for this and we are confident that the next quarter will show a considerable upturn. Once again, research and development costs were higher than expected – up from $50m to $75m. We have now stabilised that budget and don't expect any increases over the next quarters.

The marketing costs of our global campaigns for three major new products also exceeded the budget and we did in fact need $123m. But we are very pleased with projected sales figures for the products in question and marketing costs will fall drastically over the next quarters, where we will see a very healthy return on that investment. However, the immediate impact is a slight dip in trading profit to $507m.

We are, however, paying the dividend we promised to shareholders of $95m – which works out at 50 cents a share. This leaves us with a retained profit of $422m. This figure will increase considerably over the next quarters.

Unit 8 Listening 2 page 69

Speaker one

I bought shares in NavTech in 1998 at €50 a share. At that time, nobody knew that they had invented, (you know), just made up two thirds of their revenue based on a non-existent company in Hong Kong! In 1999 they went up to €60 and I was quite happy with my investment. The share price stayed the same until the scandal broke in 2001 and by 2002, my shares were worth €5 each! Imagine – 97 per cent of their declared earnings came from the imaginary company that their auditor never checked!

Speaker two

Even though the shares I bought in 1999 were terribly expensive, €115 each, I had total confidence that Com.TV would just get better and better. Little did I know that they were in fact losing millions every day on expensive loss-making acquisitions. I saw the share price fall to €80 in 2000, €50 in 2001, €40 in 2002. I kept waiting for the price to go back up again before selling, but by 2003 they were still only worth €45, so I decided to cut my losses and sell anyway.

Unit 8 Listening 3 page 73

From 1992 to 1995 there was a downturn in prices and they fell from $36 to $28. From 1995 to 1998 the value of shares started its spectacular ascension to $48 and continued to skyrocket till it reached a record high of $63 in 1999, and then, nosedived to an all time low of $7 in 2002.

Unit 8 Decision page 74

Well, of course, there are various options here but every option would obviously consider cutting the

€400,000 in the HR budget, as the freeze on recruitment means they no longer need the services of a recruitment agency. I would also reduce bonuses to €100,000 until performance picks up. Without making any redundancies, if we don't replace anyone who naturally leaves the company, I think we can expect salaries to fall by €200,000. So, that's a saving of €900,000 on the HR budget.

Some people may opt for increasing the low-quality cheap imported raw materials to reduce the production budget. This, of course, would mean downgrading from the current top-of-the-range image and therefore reduce prices and income. In fact, I think I would go back to the previous year's percentage of high-quality raw materials and reduce the cheap imported stuff with a view to improving quality. I'd also look to return to the previous year's running costs of €600,000. This would all result in the same total production budget of €3m – so no savings there.

Then, I'd cut €400,000 off the budget for advertising new products and invest €100,000 of that saving into advertising for existing products. Bringing that budget up to €250,000 and helping to concentrate on promoting our current successful brands. Finally, I'd leave the market research budget as it is – it's vital for future product development. So, that generates a saving of €300,000 on sales and marketing and an overall saving of €1.2m, or 15 per cent.

Unit 9   Listening 1 page 76

Job interviews can generally be divided into three main types. The first is what I would call the 'traditional interview'. This is usually just a series of standard questions about qualifications, work experience, knowledge and expectations. So what you have here is basically a list of quite straightforward questions, you know, like 'What duties did you have in your previous job?' This is still the model for a lot of interviews today. In my view it's not the best to select staff. In fact I would say that it's very often quite inappropriate.

Then there's the 'case interview' which is particularly challenging. What happens here is that the interviewer presents a problem and then follows this with a series of questions to find out how the candidate would approach the problem. To give you an idea, it might go something like this: 'Company X wants to increase the number of university graduates that it hires every year by 50 per cent without exceeding its current budget, which is $2m. What would you advise them to do?' Now this puts the candidate in a pretty uncomfortable position because they're really being asked to do several things – to demonstrate that they can analyse the problem logically, formulate appropriate questions and communicate effectively with the interviewer. So it's a pretty stressful form of interview.

The third type is what's known as the 'behavioural interview'. It's designed to find out how candidates actually behave in certain situations. The questions are usually based on anecdotes from the candidate's own past. They're designed to find out about how the candidates handled tricky situations and relationships in the past. A typical question might be 'Can you give me an example of a situation where you had to follow orders that you didn't agree with?' Now that puts the pressure on the candidate because they have to find a good example and they have to do the talking, so it opens up a lot of information and the interviewer gets to see more of the person who's sitting opposite.

Unit 9   Listening 2 page 80

I see that you're currently employed as assistant marketing manager at Phoenix Media. Now, as part of your job, I see you have to conduct in-depth market surveys. Can you give me an example of a recent survey that you have done and explain how you went about it?

Could you tell me a little more about exactly what you did at the media events? You say that you made presentations of company products. Was this just to customers visiting your stand or was this to a larger audience?

During your time with MSV you were responsible for some quite routine tasks like order processing. Did you enjoy doing this type of work?

At university I see that you chose to study sociology and politics as options. Can you tell me why?

You seem to be quite at home with computer technology and programming in several applications such as HTML. What sort of web-based material have you actually developed?

When you say that your level in Italian is proficient, does that mean that you would actually be able to conduct business in that language?

You obviously like sports. But I see that your interests such as horse riding and snowboarding are solitary activities, aren't they? Do you play any team sports at all?

Unit 9   Decision page 82

Well, in this case what you have is really a sort of mechanical approach to recruitment. So in many ways an interview situation like this where the time factor is critical is going to impose limitations on the interviewer and it's not going to be possible to explore the candidate's responses in great depth. In 30 minutes I don't think you can really expect to get through more than about six or eight questions. The way I think I'd approach this would be to decide which are the critical skills areas to examine in the context of service industry positions. I would say the first area is 'service awareness' – how good is the person going to be at dealing with customers, how well will he or she work within a team – next is 'security' and by that I basically mean trustworthiness. Then I think attitudes to authority and, of course, problem solving. So I would ask questions about each of those areas and then complete the interview with a question about career ambitions and one about how the candidate reacts under stress. I would evaluate each of the responses on a scale of 1–5.

Unit 10   Listening 1 page 86

One

You have to admit counterfeiting benefits consumers, particularly in developing countries, by giving them access to lower-price goods, such as medicines, that they might not otherwise be able to afford. Anyway, some brands are just so overpriced I think it's great to get almost the same quality for much less than those ridiculously high prices they charge.

Two

I think the costs of counterfeiting far outweigh the benefits. Think of the enormous cost to companies who make clothing, toys, software and pharmaceuticals and the unemployment caused by it. I mean 17,120 jobs were lost in the European Union in just one year due to competition from cheaper counterfeits. The branded industries need to invest huge amounts in research and development, marketing and advertising, which counterfeiters don't, of course. That's why branded goods are more expensive.

Unit 10   Listening 2 page 90

Well actually, you know, people in the music industry are feeling more optimistic than they have done for years, at the moment. They started to get hopeful when they managed to close down Napster in 2002, but then other file-sharing systems just took over. The pleasant surprise they've had recently is the success of Apple's iTunes Music Store, a pay online service which outperformed all expectations. It sold a million downloads in the first month of operating and after six months it had sold about 14m – totally unexpected. Add to that Napster 2, another pay for music service which has even more songs than iTunes, and it's doing very well also.

But that doesn't mean the industry's problems are over. Even if digital sales of downloads grow twentyfold, they will still only account for six per cent of the global market. Some forecasts predict that illegal file-sharing will deprive the industry of $4.7bn of revenues in 2008. They need to do something and filing lawsuits against file- sharers isn't going to solve their problems.

The illegal file-sharing networks can guard the identity of users nowadays, and anyway, every lawsuit makes their customers unhappy. Hey, this is a business like any other business – they have to think about their client base – it's time they made fundamental policy changes.

If I asked our readers why they downloaded music, you can be sure the answer would be 'because CDs are too expensive'. Obviously they have to come down in price. That's what the industry's customers are telling them by downloading free music.

I suspect another reason they are doing badly is because they aren't producing music people think is worth buying! They spend a fortune marketing music and people who have a short shelf life. What other business does that and expects long-term sales! They should drop reality TV stars for a start! They mean high investment for low returns.

On the other hand, Eminem sold ten million copies of his album *The Eminem Show* even though it can be easily downloaded on the net. Musicians with long-term sales expectations are the only ones to back, in my opinion.

Unit 11   Listening 1 page 98

A   At the moment we're doing a special offer on our top-of-the-range laptops. Would you be interested?

B   We'll see. I think we should discuss prices first.

A   Well, you know, they've only been on the market for a year and they're still retailing for

£1,500. But I can let you have them at ten per cent discount.

B   There's no way we can afford that. You'll have to make me a better offer than that!

A   OK. Let's see what we can do. How many would you need?

B   We'll need at least ten. Why don't you give us 20 per cent off? We could work with that.

A   I'm afraid I can't do that. You know they're worth more than that!

B   OK. How about 15 per cent? And we'll pay you in three instalments. We'll also need a two year warranty.

A   Well, I don't know about that. Let's say we make that 13 per cent. I'll give you the warranty and you can pay half in advance and the rest in two months.

B   OK. That's fine. When can you deliver?

Unit 11 Listening 2 page 99

I don't think selling online is really that different from selling anywhere else actually – because in both cases you're aiming to persuade customers to buy. So you have to start with the A of the famous AIDA formula – get the *attention* of the buyer. Now on an auction site that's critical because there are so many other goods listed that you've got to make your product or service stand out from the rest of the pack. So you really need a good title for the ad that's going to describe what you're selling. Remember to keep it short and to include the keywords that buyers will be using when they search.

Once you've done that, then you have to arouse their *interest* in what you're selling – and that's where the 'I' comes in – so you need to write a good description of what it is you're offering. Something that's going to make them want to acquire your product. Photos are a must! You should put in maybe four different shots of the product. That'll give buyers the impression that they've actually seen it up close.

OK, so you still haven't sold anything so far but you can help the process along by adding some sort of promotional offer – a discount on shipping or something. Give the buyer the impression you're giving them something extra for free. That builds on the D for *desire*.

The next stage is the *action* stage which is when your customer actually bids. But remember – even when you've sold your item, you still need to close the sale and that means: one – getting your money, and two – converting the buyer into someone who is going to remember you and even become a repeat customer. And the more of those you have, the easier it'll be for you to build a solid customer base with long-term relationships.

Unit 11 Decision page 100

I think that in a negotiation of this sort it's very important for both sides to understand what is at stake. And that means both companies have to consider both the long- and short-term implications for their businesses.

For N-Vision it's clearly in their interests to build a long-term relationship and to generate repeat business, so they have to be prepared to make some concessions on price, without going too far, of course. The area in which they have the greatest flexibility to improve on their offer is training – and they might even consider providing this free of charge. So, if they were to negotiate on that basis, with a ten per cent discount on all items, that would mean that Watermark would only be paying almost €12,000 for a top-of-the-range solution. On the payment side, however, I think they should stand their ground because this is the first time they have done business with Watermark and they need that guarantee.

For Watermark, one of the questions is to know if they have staff with adequate computer skills – if that's the case then they might be able to make some significant savings. Perhaps by arranging to buy their own server for less than what N-Vision is proposing. They would also need less in the way of training and they could certainly negotiate lower fees in that area, too. In my view, Watermark would be wrong to opt for a cheap solution – this site could be a critical part of their business in the future and that means they need quality and, of course, quality doesn't come cheap. So my advice to them would be not to go for the shared server option. Otherwise, well obviously, they should negotiate for whatever they can get in terms of discounts, but I don't think they can reasonably expect to reach a deal without paying at least one-third upfront.

Unit 12 Listening 1 page 102

One

I decided to join Global Exchange in their street protests because I believe you can force people to change their actions by demonstrating peacefully. You can draw their attention to the harm they may be doing and the good they could do if they changed policy. I mean, look at Starbucks. We believe that our peaceful demos outside their cafés influenced their decision to make fair trade agreements with their coffee suppliers. That guarantees coffee growers a reasonable price for their coffee and avoids unfair exploitation of coffee farmers.

Two

Our lobby group really started to affect change when we joined up with UNITE, the textile workers' union, as well as some other pressure groups, to take some of the powerful clothes companies such as Gap and Calvin Klein to court. It was wonderful when most of them decided to do something about the sweatshop working conditions and poor salaries of their employees in the third world.

Three

The lobby group Jubilee 2000 succeeded in putting the problem of third world debt at the top of the global political agenda. By the end of the campaign, they had gathered 25 million signatures and, as a result, several rich countries had promised to cancel billions of dollars of debts owed to them by the world's poorest countries. *Marie Claire* magazine helped generate public interest by publishing photos of famous people like Muhammad Ali, Star Wars actor Ewan McGregor and U2's Bono, modelling Armani-designed 'Drop the debt' T-shirts. That really helped to get young people interested in the cause.

Unit 12   Listening 2 page 106

If you want to have an impact on people and raise maximum funds, you need to plan your media campaign very carefully. There are three main outcomes to aim for. Firstly, you want to increase understanding about the needs of the people you aim to help. Then, you want to generate interest and commitment from local leaders and politicians. And finally, you need to mobilise people to either give money and/or their time to the campaign.

So, it's really important to develop a key message to achieve these aims. You have to spend research time collecting information in order to build a strong case for your work in the community. The key message has to do two things.

Firstly, it has to state the size and effects of the problem. Let's say ... the effects of living alone on a very low income ... like many of the people we care for.

What's more, you also need to show people how they can make a difference by telling success stories, showing the difference visits can make or how we can sometimes pay unpaid bills, for example. You know, human interest stories.

Then, of course, you have to prepare a news release. You see, if you get media coverage, it will be based on the news releases you send to local radio, television or newspapers. It's quite a difficult task but I find it helps to ask yourself the following questions: Will the story interest my intended audience? This is so important today as people get so many appeals for help and, therefore, to succeed, yours has to catch their attention.

If published, will it advance my ... *our* objectives? Basically, if not, why are you doing it?

And are all the facts and figures in the story 100 per cent accurate? Because, if you exaggerate or make false claims it will only generate bad publicity for your charity, and this will do more harm than good in the long run.

Unit 12   Listening 3 page 107

1 A You know how I feel about the 35-hour working week.
  B Yes, but don't you think your quality of life is much better when you work less?
  A I'm an employer and all I know for sure is that output would suffer.
  B I'm not so sure, I mean it's obvious that the quality of the actual work done improves when people work fewer hours.

2 A I would never make my restaurant completely non-smoking. I'd lose too many customers.
  B Really? Have you considered what happened in New York?
  A Why, what happened?
  B Business in restaurants actually increased when the anti-smoking laws were introduced.

3 A I'm not crazy about the euro.
  B Oh, but you must agree it's really practical when travelling in Europe.
  A Yeah, but it's really boring that so many European countries have the same money.
  B I think you've forgotten that each country has its own version with distinctive symbols on the coins.

4 A I have never understood why people invest on the stock market; it's so risky.
  B But surely you can see why people do? The higher the risk, the more money you earn.
  A And the more you lose.
  B It's been proven that in the long run, you don't lose.

Unit 13 Listening 1 page 115

Part one

I would like to start by talking about the advantages of email. I know many of you who receive hundreds of not always relevant emails a week sometimes wish it had never been invented! But let's not forget that, in comparison with other means of communication, email really is a wonderful way to keep in contact with customers and colleagues.

Firstly, email is cheaper and faster than a traditional letter – which is now known as snail mail. Email is less intrusive than a phone call, especially as people are now constantly interrupted on their cell phones. It's much less trouble than using a fax machine which is very often not in your office. Furthermore, differences in location and time zone are less an obstacle to information with email.

And finally, there is conclusive evidence that email leads to a more democratic structure, allowing all computer users easy access to company information and documents.

Part two

In today's world of information overload, getting your email read has to be your first objective. The flood of unwanted email petitions, jokes and spam means that your message could get deleted before it is even opened if you don't get your subject line right.

Subject lines should be brief, they don't need to be a full sentence. More importantly, they should contain clues to the content of the message. Lastly, you should put 'urgent' in the subject line if time is limited and if you know the person receives a lot of email.

Unit 13 Listening 2 page 116

You have six new calls. First call. Received yesterday at 8:15 pm.

Jack, how are you? Philip here, Philip Jones. Hope you had a nice weekend. Yeah, listen, I'm meeting José Dominquez next Tuesday, for lunch at 'Chez Paul' – great fish restaurant, at noon. Do you want to come? I think he will interest you. Let me know, talk to you later.

Second call. Received today at 8:57 am.
Jack, Mary Black here, I'm running a little late. My train was delayed by 20 minutes. I wouldn't mind but I got here in more than enough time. Ah well, can't be helped, I suppose. I'll be there as soon as I can.

Third call. Received today at 9:04 am.
This is Jean-Paul Cartier. I can't come to Britain next week after all. I am really very sorry. Can you phone me at my Paris number which is 1 80 54 6620 tomorrow morning. I'm not in my office today, to make another appointment.

Fourth call. Received today at 9:23 am.
Jack, Nigel Banks from finance. Have you finished the monthly accounts yet? We need them asap? I'll be here all day.

Fifth call. Received today at 9:29 am.
Good morning, my name is José Dominquez. Philip Jones gave me your number. I will be in Britain next week. I hope we can meet then. I will call you back later today. Thank you. Bye.

Sixth call. Received today at 9:41 am.
Jack, it's me again, the train is now stuck on the line between two stations! I've no idea how long we'll be here. We'd better cancel this morning. Will you call me back on my mobile when you get this message? Thanks. And I'm really very sorry. Next time I'll take the car.

Unit 13 Listening 3 page 117

1 It went really, really well; the restaurant, the meal, the service and everything were all excellent *but the thing was* we spent the whole time telling jokes. I couldn't stop laughing ... he said he'd never had such a good evening out with suppliers.

2 It wasn't exactly a holiday, you know; the sessions started at nine every morning and we didn't get out till late most evenings, *but the important point is* we really did learn a lot about project management and how to prioritise tasks and filter out unimportant information.

3 I thought it would never end, people kept getting off the point and *they went on and on* about how the hand drier in the toilets is broken, for about half an hour! It wasn't exactly on the agenda, was it! I couldn't believe it.

4 Well, actually the whole presentation was really very enjoyable and interesting but *basically, what she said was* the best strategy against infoglut was to get a good assistant to deal with most of the paperwork.

5 Well, I reckon he's leaving soon. I mean, don't tell anyone I told you, but when I asked him about arranging a date for my appraisal meeting, *he told me that* he didn't think he'd be doing it!

Part one

The smart tag is a wonderful invention which is changing the world of logistics. Managing the supply chain is so much easier with this excellent tracking technology. First of all, we can locate lost products easily, which speeds up transport time considerably. Secondly, there will be no more problems with products which have passed their sell-by dates on the shelves, because the products will inform the retailers in time! And that's not all! The new smart products will be able to communicate with the consumers. Imagine, for example, ice cream which can tell you if your refrigerator's temperature is too high!

But the most incredible of all is that finally we will be able to eliminate checkout labour altogether. Customers will just walk out of the supermarket with their shopping, and their accounts will be automatically billed. No more packing and paying at the checkout. That's going to make shopping so much easier.

Part two

J1: You refer to eliminating checkout staff, as an advantage for consumers. But surely it's all about reducing the retailer's costs. And what's going to happen to all the checkout staff?

Kate: Well yes, naturally it will reduce the industry's costs but this will also benefit consumers as retailers will lower their prices as a result.

J2: I don't think I really understand how it will work, I mean, if smart tags mean no checkout and the customer being billed automatically, won't there be a huge number of incorrect bills? And how can they be checked later?

Kate: I'm glad you mentioned that. The real advantage, you see, is that the articles you buy will be tagged and scanned as you pass through the checkout area. No more lines, no more waiting, just pop in and pop out. A whole new shopping experience!

J1: Surely the customer will have to give credit card or bank details to the retailer for this system to work. And in that case, what guarantees are there that no one else could get access to that information? What is the retailing industry planning to do about it?

Kate: We've given a great deal of thought to this. Naturally we recommend that all retailers use secure servers and protect their systems. It will be much safer than buying over the internet, for example, which consumers do very easily nowadays. I'm quite confident that most customers will not object. One more question, please.

J3: I'm much more concerned about the whole 'Big Brother' aspect of this. Retailers will be able to track consumers' movements long after they've left the store. What are you going to do to protect consumer privacy?

Kate: We're very aware of consumer fears. We are currently carrying out an in-depth study on the subject and have drawn up a list of recommendations which are in the press release. Thank you very much for coming.

Part three

The civil liberties groups think that all tagged items should have clear notices on them, specifying that they are tagged products, and that the tags themselves should be on the packaging rather than the products. This way the tracking device is thrown away with the packaging. They also believe that the tags should be clearly visible and easily removable.

1 I'm very glad you asked that question. Very important indeed, can it wait till the end? I'm sure things will be a lot clearer by then.

2 As I had gone as far as I could down that career path, I needed to find new goals and new challenges to develop and improve my skills.

3 I'm afraid I can't find any record of your order. Could you give me the invoice number and the exact date of the order and I'll get back to you?

4 I realise the recent unemployment figures are of great concern to many people right now, but you have to remember that this government has created more jobs than any other in the last 25 years.

5 I can't say how much changing the design will cost, but do you really think it's sensible to consider doing so at this late stage?

6 Despite the recent fall in share price, the company remains confident that its strategy is absolutely correct in the current trading environment and that it will be well-placed to take full advantage of any economic upturn.

Jonathan Ive is one of the most influential designers working today. He's only 37 years old and is one of the youngest designers to have won the Design

Museum's 'Designer of the Year' award, which he received in 2003. Jonathan studied design at Newcastle Polytechnic and, after graduating in 1989, he went to work for the London design agency, Tangerine. Tangerine were contacted to work on some new designs for Apple Computer, the US computer manufacturer, and in 1992 they invited Jonathan to move to their headquarters in Cupertino, California, to take up a full-time position.

Ive has been associated with a series of highly successful designs for Apple, ranging from the original iMac, with its distinctive coloured housing, which was followed by a similarly colourful laptop – the iBook, to the more recent iPod – the portable music player which has sold more than two million units since its launch two years ago.

His success is mainly due to his revolutionary approach to computer design, which has changed them from industrial machines in beige boxes into sleek, stylish fashion objects. Walk into any office and you can see in a flash which desks have Apple computers on them – they just stand out, they attract your eye and, of course, the people who use them wouldn't swap them for anything else.

Trevor Bayliss, on the other hand, has had a very unusual career path. In fact, at 15 he was a member of the national swimming team. Then he spent some time in the army, got a job as a salesman with Purley Pools, a swimming pool manufacturer, worked as a stuntman on television and then finally went on to become one of the UK's best-known inventors. He's won a number of awards for his creations including the BBC Design Award, which he received in 1996.

I think it's true to say that Trevor is more of an inventor than a designer, because he has really created a range of products that just didn't exist before. Eccentric, I suppose, would be one way to describe him, but I don't think anybody would underestimate the importance of the things he's designed. Trevor has almost single-handedly bridged part of the gap that separates the economically developed world from the developing world, by providing machines that can connect to modern sources of information, but without necessarily having to have the infrastructure that otherwise would have been necessary. Probably the most famous of these is the wind-up radio, but also the wind-up flashlight and more recently the 'electric shoe'.

Unit 15 Listening 2 page 133

1 A Great job! That was one of the most successful negotiations we've ever done and I just can't believe it all worked out so well.

B Well, thanks Sandie, but you know we had a great team working with us and we all knew that if we got this one right, then it would be good for everyone. So we had the motivation!

A Maybe. But all the same – I don't think anyone here really expected it to go that well. I'm delighted.

2 A There are just a couple of things that I am a little concerned about. I think you know we've had some problems with the quality of the software and that was really your responsibility.

B Well, that's true but it's been pretty difficult recently and we've been under a lot of pressure to get several projects finished.

A Yeah, I know but I still think you could have organised things better. And what about quality control? What went wrong there?

3 A Overall, I'd say your team did a reasonably good job and you did manage to finish the design on time.

B I think people were pretty happy with what we did.

A Well, yeah. But I think in the future we need to reduce the number of modifications that have to be made before production. Maybe you need to reorganise your team a little?

Unit 15 Decision page 134

Well, I think there are a number of factors that you have to bear in mind when you are judging this sort of competition. What I'd be looking for is a coherent, well-structured presentation, which shows the team have thought their project through in detail.

First of all, they need to show they've done the groundwork – to show there's a potential market for what they want to create. Then, that they've done enough research into similar products and services that may already exist. Next, they'd need to show a good understanding of what the cost of their project will be. And finally, they'd need a timescale for how long it will take for investors to get a return on their investment. It's only really once you get a clear picture of all those aspects that you are really in a position to select a winner.